The Addictions Recovery Workbook

101 Practical Exercises
For
Individuals and Groups

Second Edition

James E. Phelan, MSW, BCD, ICADC, Psy.D

Published by *The Practical Applications Network*

First Edition, 2007

Library of Congress Control Number: 2006905438
ISBN: 978-0-9779773-1-4

Earn CEUs from this book at:
www.GenesisCE.org

To the late, Fr. John H. Miller (1920-2006) for believing in me.

About the Author

James E. (Jim) Phelan received his doctorate degree in Psychology (Psy.D) from the Southern California University for Professional Studies and his master's degree in Social Work (MSW) from Marywood University. Jim is a Board Certified Diplomate in Clinical Social Work (BCD) and an Internationally Certified Alcohol and Drug Abuse Counselor (ICADC). He is a Research and Psychotherapist Associate to the American Psychoanalytic Association and Mental Health Affiliate to the National Association for the Advancement of Psychoanalysis. He is also a military veteran having served in both the U.S. Army and the U.S. Air Force.

James E. Phelan, MSW, BCD, ICADC, Psy.D.,
6031 E. Main Street
Suite 117
Columbus, Ohio 43213

jpmphelan@sbcglobal.net

The Addictions Recovery Workbook:
Practical Exercise for Individuals and Groups

Table of Contents

	Page
Introduction	iv
Exercise	Page
# 1: Give a complete history	1
# 2: Addiction inventory	9
# 3: Setting the stage: Daily plan for recovery	10
# 4: Daily tracker	11
# 5: Finding a sponsor/mentor	12
# 6: Write your story	13
# 7: Tell and listen to your story	14
# 8: Avoiding the media traps	15
# 9: Internet: Keep integrity online	16
#10: Spirituality	17
#11: Bibliotherapy	18
#12: Boundary inventory	19
#13: Fixing boundary violations	20
#14: Identifying and processing early childhood sexual boundaries	21
#15: Defining your relationships	22
#16: Fly in the "V" formation	23
#17: Confront the abusers	24
#18: Inner child work	25
#19: Cleaning the house	26
#20: Making and listening to affirmation tapes	27
#21: Retrain your brain	28
#22: Identifying and fixing your triggers	29
#23: Sex/Masturbation inventory	30
#24: Practice safe driving	31
#25: Accountability	32
#26: HALT	33
#27: Disputing negative self-talk	34
#28: Identifying and destroying the bad habits in thinking	35
Worksheet	36
#29: Identifying and expressing your feelings	37
#30: Improving communication skills	38
#31: Are you passive, aggressive?	39
#32: Turning threats into rewards	40
#33: How do you describe yourself?	41
#34: Pick their brain	42

Exercise	Page
#35: Writing an unfinished business letter	43
#36: Surviving the riptides	44
#37: Role reversal	45
#38: Dialoguing with your addiction	46
#39: Map for the future	47
#40: Getting your needs met	48
#41: Check out your response system	49
#42: Moving from unrealistic expectations to realistic expectations	51
#43: Let the feelings flow	52
#44: Try new activities often	53
#45: Monitoring your anger response	54
#46: Interpreting anger	55
#47: What can I do about my anger?	56
#48: Cue-controlled relaxation	57
#49: Photo analysis	58
#50: Questioning the acting out motives	59
#51: What my addiction took and takes from me	60
#52: Picture this	61
#53: Understanding your childhood roles	62
#54: My relationship with my father	63
#55: My relationship with my mother	64
#56: My relationship with my brother	65
#57: My relationship with my sister	66
#58: Control	67
#59: Forgiving Others	68
#60: No more "poor me's"	69
#61: Know thy self	70
#62: Keep a diary/journal	71
#63: Fighting self-pity with humor (hyperdramatization)	72
#64: Assessing the now and then	73
#65: Healing shame	74
#66: Understanding narcissism	76
#67: Understanding denial and other defense mechanisms	77
#67a. Looking at the denial around my addiction	80
#68: Grief work	81
#69: Tagging procrastination	82
#70: Inventory on how my addiction impacts others	83
#71: Assertiveness	84
#72: Understanding group dynamics	85
#73: Rules for getting the most out of group	86
#74: Talking to the group	87
#75: Opening up in a recovery group	88
#76: Topics to talk about in group	89

Exercise	Page
#77: Group work on the topic of boundaries	90
#78: Relapse warning signs	91
#79: Relapse prevention plan	93
#80: Recovery plan outline	96
#81: Recovery plan worksheet	102
#82: Looking at addictive behaviors: Inside and outside perspectives	105
#83: Honesty about my addiction	106
#84: What causes me emotional pain	107
#85: Keeping a mood log	108
#86: Building trust	109
#87: Getting real	110
#88: Journaling	111
#89: Relieving boredom	112
#90: Mirroring	113
#91: Identifying old rules: Rule no more!	114
#92: Surrendering to reality	115
#93: "Hugs not drugs" (or other addictions)	116
#94: Sleep	117
#95: Social life affirmation	118
#96: Dealing with your fear of failure	119
#97: Centering	120
#98: Nurturing yourself	121
#99: Asking for forgiveness	122
#100: Good-bye letter to your addiction	123
#101: Final Exercise - Become a champion for change	124
Bibliography	125
Appendix A: Feelings list	127
Appendix B: Activities list	130
Appendix C: Communication: Speaker-listener checklist	135
Appendix D: Addictions Inventory	136

Suggested Exercises for Various Subtopics

Anger
#17, 45, 46, 47

Assessment/Inventories
#1, 2, 14, 22, 23, 28, 29, 31, 33, 39, 61, 64, 70

Behavioral Modification
#4, 8, 9, 13, 16, 19, 22, 23, 24, 26, 30, 41, 44, 58, 69, 71

Cognitive (Thinking) Restructuring
#11, 27, 28, 32, 38, 42, 58, 60, 61, 67

Family
#4, 9, 53, 54, 55, 56, 57

Feelings
#6, 7, 18, 29, 35, 38, 43, 68

Specific to Group Work
#72, 73, 74, 75

Recovery Plans
#3, 78, 79

Relapse Prevention
#5, 25, 26, 76, 77

Relational Healing
#5, 10, 13, 14, 15, 16, 17, 18, 40

Introduction

First off, let me congratulate you for taking this courageous step forward in your recovery! The exercises you are about to complete are geared toward both behavioral modification and affect regulation. This workbook is not intended to be used solely as a self-help book, but rather to be used to accompany counseling, group work, or sponsorship. It's best to process these exercises with someone. That "someone" should be a counselor, sponsor, mentor, or clergy who is trained in and familiar with the recovery of your addiction. Addictions do not only mean chemical dependency such as drugs and alcohol, but sex, eating, relationships, spending, working, or gambling just to name a few.

These exercises present an inherent challenge to your healing process. Sponsorship or mentorship is also very important in the recovery of addictions, regardless of your age. You should not forgo recovery alone. You should have a basic foundation in recovery prior to beginning this workbook. You must keep that motivation for change and be committed to following through. If not, success will not accompany.

The 1997 version of the movie *Titanic* cost over 200 million dollars to produce, making it the most expensive movie ever made to that date. However, the movie grossed over 1.8 billion dollars! Recovery takes a lot of time and energy, but in the long run, it is well worth it. Like making the movie *Titanic*, when much is put in, much greater is gained.

Herein are many exercises, therefore be cautious to not get overwhelmed by them all. Instead, slowly process through each one. They are appropriate for individual and/or group use. I have included *suggested readings* so that you can expand your support arena. You will find it easier to use a separate notebook to process your work as space is limited within the confines of the book. I recommended that you start each day with the exercise, "Setting the stage: Daily plan for recovery" (Exercise #3) and then choose any one numbered exercise to work on. Some exercises may only take a short while to complete while others may take several days and even months to complete. Be patient! I have grouped some exercises into subtopics (see page iv) making it easier for you choose which exercise to work on. Please note that the numbered exercises are not in any particular order for completion.

At last, I wish you the greatest success in your healing journey!

~Jim

Look to this day,
For it is life,
In its brief course lie all
The realities and verities of existence,
The bliss of growth,
The splendor of action,
The glory of power

For yesterday is but a dream,
And tomorrow is only a vision,
But today, well lived,
Makes every yesterday a dream
Of happiness
And every tomorrow a vision of hope.

Look well, therefore, to this day.

SANSKRIT PROVERB

Exercise # 1

Give a complete history

Complete the follow questionnaire. The format is comprehensive, yet helpful as it assists you to really think about many life facets. Process this with someone who is working with you in your recovery.

Name: (Last) ____
First: ____

Today's date ______/______/_____ Who referred you? ___________________________________

Your Address: ____
City/Town: ___________________________ State: _________ ZIP: __________

Phone: Work ( ) _____________________________
Home ( ) _____________________________________

Cell ( ) _______________________ Pager ( ) ________________
E-mail: ____

Date of birth: ____/______/______ Current Age: _________
Place of birth: ____

Social security number: ___________________________ Nationality: [ ] U.S. [ ] Other (specify): ______________________

Gender: [ ] Male [ ] Female
Race: [ ] Caucasian [ ] African American [ ] Hispanic [ ] Asian [ ] Other: __________________

Marital status: [ ] Single, Never Married [ ] Married [ ] Separated [ ] Divorced [ ] Widowed

Current living situation: [ ] alone [ ] with spouse/mate [ ] with parents [ ] with siblings [ ] Other:

In what religion were you raised: [ ] None [ ] Protestant [ ] Catholic [ ] Jewish
[ ] Other (specify): ____

What religion are you now: [ ] None [ ] Protestant [ ] Catholic [ ] Jewish
[ ] Other (specify): ____

Ethnic background of your mother's family: ____

Ethnic background of your father's family: ____

EMERGENCY CONTACT Name: ____________________________________
Relationship to you: _________________

Daytime phone: (   ) ____

Evening phone: (   ) ____
(For ER purpose only, no confidential info given unless permitted)
Your Current Occupation: ___________________________________
Position:___________________________
How long at this job?_________________

Level of satisfaction with your job: [ ] excellent [ ] good [ ] fair [ ] poor

YOUR EDUCATION & TRAINING (Start w/ most recent)

School or Facility	Dates Attended	Degree	Major Area of Study

Substance	Age of First Use	Time Since Last Use	Currently a "Problem"? (3)	Ever a "Problem" ? (3)	Longest time able to remain abstinent from this drug when you were deliberately trying to stop using it.
Cocaine snorting (powder)					
Cocaine smoking (crack)					
Methamphetamine					
Alcohol					
Heroin					
Methadone					
Prescription Opioids *Specify*:					
Marijuana					
Benzodiazepines					
Barbiturates					
Hallucinogens (LSD)					
"Ecstacy" (MDMA)					
Amyl Nitrate "Snappers"					
"Special K" (ketamine)					

Substance	Age of First Use	Time Since Last Use	Currently a "Problem"? (3)	Ever a "Problem"? (3)	Longest time able to remain abstinent from this drug when you were deliberately trying to stop using it.
PCP "Angel Dust"					
Steroids					
Rohypnol "Roofies"					
GHB "G"					
Nitrous Oxide/ "Whippets"					
Other (specify)					

YOUR HISTORY OF SUBSTANCE USE

YOUR ALCOHOL & DRUG USE DURING THE PAST FIVE DAYS

	SUBSTANCES USED	AMOUNTS USED
Today		
Yesterday		
2 days ago		
3 days ago		
4 days ago		

Which substance do you consider to be your primary drug of choice ?
[ ] Alcohol [ ] Cocaine [ ] Marijuana [ ] Heroin [ ] Methamphetamine [ ] Ecstasy [ ] Nitrous Oxide
[ ] Prescription Opioids (specify) [ ] Prescription Tranquilizers (specify) [ ] Other (specify)

ALCOHOL USE

When you drink alcohol, what types of beverages do you most often drink? (check all that apply)
[ ] beer [ ] wine [ ] vodka [ ] gin [ ] scotch/whiskey [ ] other (specify)______________________

How many drinks do you usually have ? per day __________ per week __________________

Do you experience any physical problems when you try to stop drinking? [ ] No [ ] Yes, check all that apply
[ ] shakes or trembling [ ] sweating [ ] vomiting [ ] sleep problems [ ] seizures [ ] hallucinations

Have you ever experienced physical withdrawal or other medical complications from prior attempts to stop drinking alcohol?
[ ] No [ ] Yes, please describe

SUBSTANCE USE PROFILE

Have you ever found yourself thinking a great deal about alcohol/drugs or being preoccupied with using?
[ ] Yes [ ] No
Have you ever experienced cravings or a strong compulsion to use alcohol/drugs?
[ ] Yes [ ] No
Have you ever had difficulty in reducing or totally stopping your alcohol/drug use?
[ ] Yes [ ] No [ ] Never tried to stop
Have you ever used more frequently and/or in larger amounts than you intended to?
[ ] Yes [ ] No
Have you ever been under the influence of alcohol/drugs while driving a car or operating other dangerous machinery?
[ ] Yes [ ] No
Has alcohol/drug use ever caused you to miss workdays or impaired your productivity, effectiveness, or judgment at work?
[ ] Yes [ ] No
Have you ever become less sociable, socially withdrawn, or isolated as a result of using alcohol/drugs?
[ ] Yes [ ] No
Have you ever given up recreational activities, exercise, or other healthy pursuits due to alcohol/drug use?
[ ] Yes [ ] No
Has your self-esteem or self-image ever been negatively affected by your alcohol/drug use?
[ ] Yes [ ] No
Have you ever engaged in "STD risky" sexual behavior such as having sexual encounters with unknown partners or having "STD-risky" unprotected sex with someone other than your primary mate while under the influence of alcohol/drugs?
[ ] Yes [ ] No
Have relationships with a mate, family members, or significant others been damaged by your alcohol/drug use? [ ] Yes [ ] No
Have you ever used alcohol/drugs to "medicate" yourself for depression, anxiety, or other negative moods?
[ ] Yes [ ] No
Do you feel a need for professional help to deal with your alcohol/drug problem?
[ ] Yes [ ] No [ ] Not Sure

YOUR TOTAL NUMBER OF "YES" RESPONSES ____________

ANY ADDICTION/COMPLUSIONS PROFILE

Have you ever found yourself thinking a great deal about something other then substances or being preoccupied with it?
[ ] Yes [ ] NO

If so, name it:____

Have you ever experienced cravings or a strong compulsion for this?
[ ] Yes [ ] No
Have you ever had difficulty in reducing or totally stopping desire for this?
[ ] Yes [ ] No [ ] Never tried to stop
Has this ever caused you to miss workdays or impaired your productivity and/or effectiveness, at work?
[ ] Yes [ ] No

Have you ever become less sociable, socially withdrawn, or isolated as a result of this?
[ ] Yes [ ] No
Have you ever given up recreational activities, exercise, or other healthy pursuits due to this?
[ ] Yes [ ] No
Has your self-esteem or self-image ever been negatively affected by this?
[ ] Yes [ ] No
Have you ever engaged in "STD risky" sexual behavior, such as having sexual encounters with unknown partners or having "STD-risky" unprotected sex with someone other than your primary mate while under the influence of this?
[ ] Yes [ ] No
Have relationships with a mate, family members, or significant others been damaged by this?
[ ] Yes [ ] No
Have you ever used this to "medicate" yourself for depression, anxiety, or other negative moods?
[ ] Yes [ ] No
Do you feel a need for professional help to deal with this?
[ ] Yes [ ] No [ ] Not Sure

YOUR TOTAL NUMBER OF "YES" RESPONSES ____________

CONSEQUENCES OF YOUR ADDICTIONS

<u>Check all that apply during the past 3-6 months or similar period prior to any recent discharge from inpatient rehab</u>

PSYCHOLOGICAL [ ] Irritability, short temper [ ] Self-hate [ ] Depression [ ] Suicidal thoughts or actions [ ] Homicidal thoughts or actions [ ] Paranoia, suspiciousness [ ] Memory problems [ ] Anxiety or panic attacks [ ] Other (describe):

SEXUAL [ ] Loss of sexual desire[ ] Sexual obsession [ ] Sex with strangers [ ] AIDS-risky sex [ ] Inability to achieve orgasm [ ] Inability to achieve or sustain erection [ ] Other (describe):

RELATIONSHIPS [ ] Arguments with mate [ ] Violence with mate [ ] Breakup of marriage or relationship [ ] Loss of friends [ ] Arguments with parents or siblings [ ] Other (describe):

JOB OR FINANCIAL [ ] Job loss or threatened job loss [ ] Lateness or absenteeism[ ] Less productive at work [ ] In debt [ ] Falling behind in paying bills [ ] Other (describe):

LEGAL [ ] Arrested for possession of illegal drugs [ ] Arrested for sale of illicit drugs [ ] Arrested for DWI [ ] Other:

TREATMENT HISTORY

INPATIENT OR REHAB - Hospital Detox, Psychiatric Facility, or Alcohol/Drug Rehab

Facility	Reason for Admission	Admission Date	Length of Stay	Results- completed/ dropped out

OUTPATIENT SUBSTANCE ABUSE TREATMENT- Alcohol/Drug Program or Clinic

Facility	Reason for Admission	Admission Date	Length of Stay	Results- completed/ dropped out

Are you currently in treatment with a psychologist, psychiatrist, or other therapist? [ ] No [ ] Yes

Practitioner's name: ____

Primary reason for seeking help____

Seeing this clinician for how long? __________ How useful has it been for you?____________________

PRESCRIBED MEDICATIONS YOU ARE CURRENTLY TAKING:

Medication	Dose per day	Condition or Illness	Doctor's Name	Approx. starting date

SELF-HELP INVOLVEMENT

Have you ever attended a meeting of AA/CA/NA? [ ] No [ ] Yes- For how long? ______________
How often do you go to meetings now? _______________ Do you have a sponsor? [ ] Yes [ ] No

What do you like best about the meetings? What do you like least?

Please describe any <u>previous</u> self-help involvement and why you stopped going:

Please Answer <u>ALL</u> Questions Below

(Explain any YES answers)

Have you ever been hospitalized or treated in an ER for an overdose?	[ ] No	[ ] Yes
Past 30 days?	[ ] No	[ ] Yes
Have you ever had seizures, convulsions, or epilepsy?	[ ] No	[ ] Yes
Past 30 days?	[ ] No	[ ] Yes
Have you ever had blackouts (memory gaps) due to alcohol/drug use?	[ ] No	[ ] Yes
Past 30 days?	[ ] No	[ ] Yes
Have you ever felt suicidal or had repeated thoughts about harming yourself?	[ ] No	[ ] Yes
Past 30 days?	[ ] No	[ ] Yes
Have you ever planned out or chosen a specific method for killing yourself?	[ ] No	[ ] Yes
Past 30 days?	[ ] No	[ ] Yes
Have you ever attempted to kill or seriously harm yourself?	[ ] No	[ ] Yes
Past 30 days?	[ ] No	[ ] Yes
Have you ever been hospitalized due to a suicide attempt or suicidal thoughts?	[ ] No	[ ] Yes
Past 30 days?	[ ] No	[ ] Yes
Are you afraid that you might try to harm yourself in the near future?	[ ] No	[ ] Yes
Past 30 days?	[ ] No	[ ] Yes
Do you have a history of being violent toward other people?	[ ] No	[ ] Yes
Past 30 days?	[ ] No	[ ] Yes
Do you ever have persistent thoughts or fantasies about harming other people?	[ ] No	[ ] Yes
Past 30 days?		

Please explain any "YES" answers below:

DEPRESSION: OVER THE PAST 30-60 DAYS:

Have you been feeling depressed, down, blue, or hopeless on a regular basis?	[ ] No	[ ] Yes
Has your appetite significantly increased or decreased?	[ ] No	[ ] Yes
Have you lost or gained a significant amount of weight?	[ ] No	[ ] Yes
Have you experienced problems falling asleep or staying asleep on most nights?	[ ] No	[ ] Yes
Have you been sleeping too much or having trouble getting out of bed?	[ ] No	[ ] Yes
Have you been feeling worthless and/or overwhelmed with guilt?	[ ] No	[ ] Yes
Have you been feeling irritable, agitated, restless, or unable to concentrate?	[ ] No	[ ] Yes
Have you lost interest or reduced participation in pleasurable activities?	[ ] No	[ ] Yes
Have you been less interested in sex?	[ ] No	[ ] Yes
Have you been avoiding social contact or become withdrawn and isolated?	[ ] No	[ ] Yes
Have you been feeling overwhelmed with sadness or had crying spells?	[ ] No	[ ] Yes
Has your overall energy level decreased or been much lower than usual?	[ ] No	[ ] Yes
Have you been feeling that life may not be worth living?	[ ] No	[ ] Yes

Your total number of "YES" responses ______________

YOUR CHILDREN (if any)

Name	Age	School Grade Occupation	Resides where, with whom?	History of Behavior Problems	History of Alcohol/Drug Problems

YOUR FAMILY-OF-ORIGIN (if any are deceased, include year, cause, and age at time of death)

Relative	Name	Age	Occupation	History of Alcohol/Drug Abuse	History of Mental Illness	If deceased, list yr/Cause/Age
Father						
Mother						
Sibling						
Sibling						
Sibling						
Sibling						

Describe any events in your upbringing that have negatively affected your life (e.g., frequent relocations; sexual or physical abuse; parental divorce/death/chronic illness/substance abuse, etc.):

LEARNING AND BEHAVIOR PROBLEMS

Did you ever have any learning, attention, hyperactivity, or other behavior problems in school? [ ] No [ ] Yes-describe____

Were you ever diagnosed as having a [ ] learning disability [ ] attention deficit disorder [ ] hyperactivity disorder

Did you ever receive tutoring, therapy, or medication for these problems? [ ] No [ ] Yes, describe

MEDICAL

Do you have any current medical problems? [ ] No [ ] Yes, describe:____
Are you currently under a doctor's care for these problems? [ ] No [ ] Yes, name of doctor:______________________
Have you experienced any serious illness within the past year? [ ] No [ ] Yes, describe:___________________________
Please indicate whether you have EVER had any of the medical conditions listed below (check all that apply):
[ ] high blood pressure [ ] heart disease [ ] epilepsy, seizures, convulsions [ ] kidney disease
[ ] diabetes [ ] colitis [ ] thyroid disease [ ] pancreatitis [ ] cancer [ ] TB [ ] HIV [ ] Hep A
[ ] Hep B [ ] Hep C [ ] serious head or brain injury [ ] other serious illness (describe):

FINANCIAL

Are you currently experiencing financial problems? [ ] No [ ] Yes
Are you falling behind in paying: [ ] rent [ ] credit card [ ] loans [ ] car payment
Are you having to borrow money to keep up with monthly living expenses? [ ] No [ ] Yes

MILITARY

Have you ever served in the military? [ ] No [ ] Yes
If yes, did you receive an honorable discharge? [ ] Yes [ ] No, please explain:

LEGAL

Have you ever been arrested or convicted of a crime? [ ] No [ ] Yes, explain
Are there any legal charges or lawsuits pending against you? [ ] No [ ] Yes, explain

RELATIONSHIPS

Your sexual orientation: [ ] heterosexual [ ] homosexual [ ] bisexual
Are you currently involved in a significant relationship? [ ] Yes [ ] No
Name of your spouse/mate:____________________________________
Spouse/mate's Age: _______ Occupation:______________________
Current areas of conflict with your mate:
Does he/she have any history of emotional or psychiatric problems? [ ] No [ ] Yes, please explain:
Does he/she have a history of alcohol or drug problems? [ ] No [ ] Yes, please explain:

MARITAL HISTORY

How many times have you been married? _______
If currently married, for how long? _____________ Reasons for prior separation/divorce:

Which of these statements best describes how <u>you</u> see your alcohol/drug use:

[ ] My alcohol/drug use is NOT a problem
[ ] My alcohol/drug use MIGHT be a problem, but I'm not really sure
[ ] My alcohol/drug use DEFINITELY is a problem

Which of these statements best describes how <u>you</u> see any other addictions problem in your life:

[ ] It is NOT a problem
[ ] It MIGHT be a problem, but I'm not really sure
[ ] It is DEFINITELY a problem

What else might be important for someone to know about you? (Use separate pages if you need more space)

Exercise #2

The addictions inventory

Addictions vary in intensity depending on the individual. However, it is good to get an idea of where you are at. The inventory found in **Appendix D** will help you gage and understand your level of addiction. Please complete the inventory in Appendix D and see where you are at. Process the data. The results can help shape the focus and attention of your recovery process.

Complete Inventory in Appendix D

Exercise # 3

Setting the stage: Daily plan for recovery

Recovery from addictions is a tough battle. Each day is a new beginning and should be dedicated to exercise time for your recovery. I call this setting the stage. What does that look like? Actually it's pretty simple. It is asking yourself, "What am I going to do today to work on my recovery"? It is the dedication to stick to a plan. This corresponds to the old saying, "If you fail to plan, you plan to fail". Everyone is different, so the results of this particular exercise will look different for everyone. It is a dual phase approach: 1) Wake up and ask yourself: "What will I do today to aid in my recovery?" and 2) "What tools will I need?" Your tools can be a variety of people, places, and/or things. They are the mechanisms in which you will put your desires into action. Use the outline below to guide you.

1. What will I do today to work on my recovery? ______________________________

____

____

____

2. What tools do I need? ____

____

____

____

3. What is my plan of action? What exercise(s) will I work on today? _____________

____

____

____

____

Exercise # 4

Daily tracker

It is important to track the severity of your addiction during the early stages of recovery. This will help you to gage where you are at and to track patterns and trends. This daily tracker is an excellent tool for you to use and then further process with someone. Here's how it works: At the end of each day, take the time to review the severity of addiction that you have experienced over the course of the day. Severity can include things like addictive thinking and/or behaviors. Create a scale ranging from 0 to 10; whereas 10 represent the problem at its worst and zero represents no problems at all. Plot the number each day on the chart example below. Lastly, note what you did during that day to require such a rating on the scale.

Severity

10							
9							
8							
7							
6							
5							
4							
3							
2							
1							
0							
	Day 1	Day 2	Day 3	Day 4	Day 5	Day 6	Day 7

Exercise # 5

Finding a sponsor/mentor

Probably one of the most important elements of recovery and healing is sponsorship/mentoring. You cannot heal alone. One of the most difficult areas in recovery is finding the right person. One reason is that the struggler finds it hard to ask for mentoring and another is that good sponsors/mentors are hard to come by. While this combination makes it difficult, it is not impossible. This exercise is most likely a process rather than an event. Finding a mentor takes careful choosing and therefore time. A sponsor/mentor must be strong, genuine, warm, nonjudgmental, kind, yet challenging and has resolved his* own hang-ups. A man in recovery should find another man; and for the woman in recovery, another woman. In this exercise you will follow the bullets listed below. Then process how you are going to make this happen in your own life. Use the worksheet below to stage your sponsorship/mentorship:

- List up to five ideal people who can help you find a mentor/sponsor.**
- List up to five appropriate actual candidates to be your mentor/sponsor.
- List their demographics (names, locations, how long you've known them, whether or not they know about your addiction, marital status, affiliations, etc.).
- Write what you will say to your mentor/sponsor in asking them to mentor you.
- Role-play this with a safe person.

After you have chosen your mentor/sponsor(s), list the person(s) you both will be accountable to and who can also help you facilitate some processing.

* For grammatical consistency "his" "he" or "him" are used and refers to human beings of either gender. I have used these pronouns in this exercise and throughout the remainder of the book for that purpose only and no insensitivity or exclusion is intended.

** If you have trouble identifying candidates, ask for help in forming ideas from support group leaders, clergy, organizations, or other safe sources.

Exercise # 6

Write your story

It is important to be able to write about yourself and your history. The process helps you to see those details you may often set aside. In this exercise, think back to your earliest recollections. Start there. Write in chronological order your salient memories. Describe who was part of your life. Describe where you lived and what it was like. Describe your family. Talk about your school days and peers. Talk about teachers. Make sure you include both positive and negative recollections. Discuss your earliest thoughts and fantasies. Discuss how your addiction has been a part of your life and how it developed. Let this process flow. You may not be able to finish it all in one sitting and that's okay. Take your time. Finish up by mentioning where you are today. Please use a separate notebook or type it on separate pages. Process this with someone or in group.

My story:

Exercise # 7

Tell and listen to your story

In Exercise # 6, you wrote your story; now it is time to tell it. This can be a challenge, especially due to the shame that is inherent in addictions. In this exercise pick someone to listen to you. This person must be safe and nonjudgmental. He or she must be able to provide a supportive, confidential environment for you to read your words. It may help to tape-record this first. That way you can practice the process and be able to play it back and listen to it again and again.

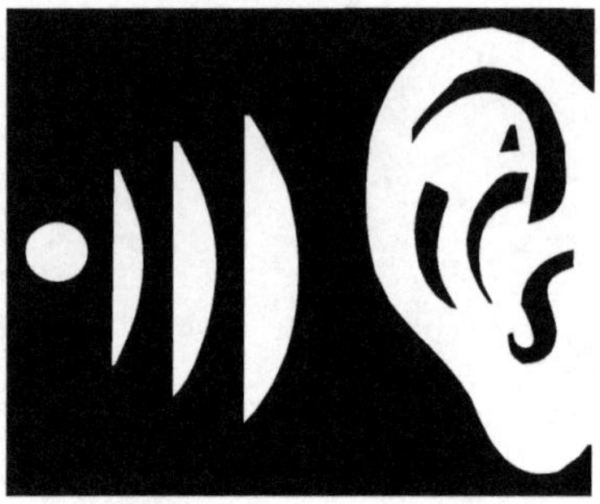

Exercise # 8

Avoiding the media traps

This is an important exercise as it helps you to win against the illusions portrayed by the entertainment industry. That environment only glorifies addictions, which is not helpful to your recovery. The media bombards you daily from many directions: TV, commercials and advertisements, radio, games, Internet*, Cams, CDs/DVDs. The problem with media in recovery is that it can fuel the fire you are trying to extinguish. It only increases urges, encourages acting out, and leads to mind games. This exercise helps you to put a cleansing to the issue.

In the inventory that follows, list the media that presents a problem for you in your recovery. Then eliminate them from your daily activities. Next to the items on the list, check them off once you have eliminated them. Process this with someone. Be accountable to them if you relapse back into any of the media on the list.

Inventory

List the media troublesome to you:	Elimination check mark
1.____	______
2.____	______
3.____	______
4.____	______
5.____	______
6.____	______
7.____	______
8.____	______

* A separate exercise has been developed specifically for the internet; see exercise # 9

Exercise # 9

Internet: Keep integrity online

The internet, our greatest technology, gets more advanced each day. It is very easy to access data to fulfill your addiction in no time at all. At the same time, the internet is helpful to advance business and professional goals. So, how do you keep the balance? In this exercise, use the following checklist and corresponding advice to keep your integrity online.

Inventory	Yes	No
Is someone other then you able to keep your system(s) accountable? If no, then see that you get accountability. Have an accountability partner check your history daily.	___	___
Do you have a filter program? If no, invest in one and keep it.	___	___
Do you keep one email address for home and one for business? Never keep a "spare address". Make sure your accountability partner has your address and you have no "secret" or "back up" addresses.	___	___
Is your address highly linked to your name? Make sure people know it is you writing; don't put on a false self.	___	___
Can you stop using the internet for 30 days? If no, maybe you are too reliant on it? Try other ways.	___	___
Do you have a spam blocker? Invest in one. Delete unsolicited or unknown emails.	___	___
Do you use your computer in private? If so, use it in a common area. Do not isolate yourself.	___	___
Do you stay up late or invest large amounts of time internet surfing? Do not use the computer for non-specific uses. Remember, in recovery, isolating activities are to be avoided.	___	___

Action Plan: ____

Exercise # 10

Spirituality

It is a well known fact that those with a higher level of spirituality do very well in their recovery. In this exercise, assess your level of spirituality and see what you can do to increase your spiritual involvement. If you are agnostic or an atheist, your exercise would be to talk with people who are spiritual and interview them. Ask them what spirituality means to them. Another exercise would be to visit a place of worship or make an appointment with a clergyman and witness the environment for yourself.

Finally, under "Goals for more involvement" (see below) for example, don't just simply write "I need more," rather write specifically what you need to do to get more involved.

Inventory & Goal Plan

Level of Involvement	Goal for more involvement
Attend worship service: (example: I go to church on Sun. mornings only)	Attend the Saturday service also.
Prayer/meditation: ______________________	______________
Reading Holy Scriptures: ______________________	______________
Study Group: ______________________	______________
Ministries: ______________________	______________
Music: ______________________	______________

Other forms of worship or spirituality: ______________________________

____

Exercise # 11

Biblotherapy

It is imperative while you are in recovery to read materials focused on addiction recovery. This is known as Biblotherapy. There are a lot of helpful materials available. I have included a bibliography at the end of this book. Please go there and review the listings. Choose a book and obtain it. Read it chapter-by-chapter while taking notes. Write down any highlights, as well as any questions you may have. Share this with someone or in a group so you can process it.

Name of material	Reading dates
______________________________	__________
______________________________	__________
______________________________	__________
______________________________	__________
______________________________	__________
______________________________	__________
______________________________	__________
______________________________	__________
______________________________	__________
______________________________	__________
______________________________	__________
______________________________	__________
______________________________	__________
______________________________	__________

Exercise # 12

Boundary inventory

Boundaries are an important aspect of recovery. During your addiction, boundaries have been blurred. In recovery, you have the opportunity to clarify boundaries and make them right. They must work to support you and to provide physical, mental, emotional, and spiritual safety. An example of a good emotional boundary is when you are able to assert yourself with others. An example of a healthy physical boundary is when you are able to make it clear to others what is predictable from you. An unhealthy physical boundary is physical intimidation, for example. In the following exercise you will inventory your boundaries and decide what changes need to occur.

1. What kind of boundaries do I have?
2. What boundaries do I need?
3. What area in my life is it the hardest to have a healthy boundary?
4. What changes would I like to make in my boundaries?
5. What do I need to do to make these changes?

Exercise # 13

Fixing boundary violations

Boundaries are necessary to create an environment that is more conducive to healing. In this exercise, identify the people with whom boundaries need to be set. Then state the boundary, which is what *you* need to do to make this work. Notice how I said, "You!" For example, if your mother is calling too often and it is making *you* uncomfortable, then that is the "boundary violation". The boundary you set, for example, would be to discuss with her that you are not going to accept her calls, that for now on *you* will initiate the calls. This will put *you* in control. Use the format below to help guide you through this process of fixing boundary violations:

Boundary violation	By whom	Boundary set
Mom calls too much.	*Mother*	*I will call her, not vice versa.*

Exercise # 14

Identifying and processing early childhood sexual boundaries

Sexuality while growing up is often confusing. If you had parents who did not help you process sexuality, boundaries could have been crossed or blurred. In this exercise, answer the following to process your childhood sexual boundaries.

[Note: If you have experienced sexual abuse, please be sure to have immediate access and close support from someone equipped to help you while doing this exercise.]

Did your parents talk to you about sex when you were growing up?

Explain how your parents talked about sex:

What sexual boundaries have been crossed growing up?

If so, when, with whom, how often?

What happened?

What have you thought about this over the years? What feelings come up?

Exercise # 15

Defining your relationships

You should have many different relationships in your life. A variety of relationships helps make you a well-rounded person. In each relationship, however, you must define the role and expectations you have about that relationship. In this exercise list each significant person in your life and the roles you expect each person to fulfill for you. For each role, list in detail the expectations you have or should have.

Person:____

Role(s):____

Expectations: ____

____

Person:____

Role(s):____

Expectations: ____

____

Person:____

Role(s):____

Expectations: ____

____

Person:____

Role(s):____

Expectations: ____

____

Exercise # 16

Fly in the "V" formation

When geese fly in a "V" formation, the whole flock adds at least 71% flying range than if each bird flew on its own. Whenever a goose falls out of the formation, it suddenly feels the drag and resistance of trying to go at it alone. People who share common direction and sense of community can get where they are going quicker and easier, because they are traveling on the thrust of one another. In this exercise you are asked to join a non-therapy, organizational group or club with emphasis on being with others. The group does not necessarily have to know about your addiction. The group can be either religious or secular.

In this exercise, list the prospective organization or club that you wish to connect with, and then list their contact information. Contact them and get the specifics. Then visit them. List the date. Once you find your niche, then highlight it and attend regularly. You're in! Enjoy!

List

Organization, Club	Contact Information	Date
______________________	______________________	_______
______________________	______________________	_______
______________________	______________________	_______
______________________	______________________	_______
______________________	______________________	_______
______________________	______________________	_______
______________________	______________________	_______
______________________	______________________	_______
______________________	______________________	_______

Exercise # 17

Confront your abusers

We have all suffered abuse in one form or fashion. The most common, but usually unrecognizable, is emotional and mental abuse. However, sexual and physical abuse are also very common with people struggling with addictions. Emotional or mental abuses have usually been reinforced by peers or siblings. Teasing and name calling are indeed abuse. You may not have seen it as such, since abuse itself is usually affiliated with beatings and molestations. But whether or not the abuse was overt or subtle, it was abuse nevertheless and it must be confronted. One of the most powerful ways to confront the abuser is to write a letter to him/or her. The letter allows you to tell the abuser how you felt during the abuse and how it has affected you. It allows you to tell the abuser that you will no longer allow him/her to have a stronghold on you. You confront him/her and tell him/her that he/she is wounded and that you wish he/she would get help. Your closing is to say that you are going to live well despite the abuse and that even though you won't forget it, you will survive it. Start your letter with, "Dear_________". If you remember the affects of the abuse but have forgotten or suppressed the abuser's name, just start with "Dear Abuser…."

You do not have to send this letter. Writing it is the real experience, however if you feel you should send it, do so. If you feel you should read it instead, that is okay too. One caution, *don't expect the abuser to react in a positive manner*. They are often filled with denial and suppression. Keep this in mind; don't allow yourself to be revictimized. Just remember the process is for you, not the abuser. It is for you to say what has been locked away for so long. You may also want to examine the role of forgiveness to see how this cuts the unhealthy ties that bind you to the abuser. See exercise # 59, "Forgiveness."

In cases where it may be dangerous to confront the abuser, you may want to do so in a controlled environment where you can arrange safety measures to be in place, or not confront directly if unsafe to do so.

Exercise # 18

Inner child work

"...even though we grow in size, that sensitive and fragile little being never disappears. Usually hidden, the child lives on and waits for us to reclaim him or her."

–Capacchione, p.69

1. Write a story about yourself as a carefree child. Write about what you liked and how you played. Write about what dreams and aspirations you had. Use your notebook to write this in.
2. Watch the movie *Big* starring Tom Hanks. Notice how he lets his inner child come out.
3. Explore your own inner child by going to a toy store or amusement park. Water parks are good choices since you get to take off and run around carefree. Write and process your experiences there.
4. Obtain the book, *Recovery of Your Inner Child* by Lucia Capacchione. The book has three sections and includes practical exercises of which you can process with someone.
5. Listen to Audio CD: *Songs for the Inner Child* by Shaina Noll or Brenda Schaeffer's CD *Inner reflections: Meditations for the body and heart*. Meditate on the words and/or music. Allow the words and/or music to nurture your inner child.

Assigned Medias for this exercise:

Read: Capacchione, L. (1991). *Recovery of your inner child.* New York: Fireside Books.
Audio: Brenda Schaeffer's CD *Inner reflections: Meditations for the body and heart.* Center City, MN: Hazelden and/or *Songs for the Inner Child* by Shaina Noll, Singing Heart, 1994.

Exercise # 19

Cleaning the house

In this practical behavioral exercise you will clean out those things around the house, office, or car that feed into your addiction. You may have already cleaned out a lot in the exercise "Avoiding the media traps," however there may be some more things around that you need to get rid of. Address and telephone books are an example. You may be holding onto phone numbers of past liaisons or "dope boys" for "just in case." Or you may think, "Maybe I can reach out and help this person one day after I am healed." Have you ever heard these before? The bottom line is that you have to clean the slate. In this exercise you will clean out your old phone numbers and address books, plus any other items that are associated with your addiction.

Cleaning list:

____

____

____

____

____

____

____

____

____

____

____

Exercise # 20

Making and listening to affirmation tapes

In this exercise you will: 1) Write a letter about how you would have liked to have been treated as a child growing up by your father, mother, siblings, and peers (or others that were involved in your life such as cousins or uncles). 2) Tape-record this in your own words or have a friend read it on the tape. Play soft music in the background. 3) Listen to the tape in a relaxed environment. Start the process by listening to Brenda Schaeffer's CD *Inner reflections: Meditations for the body and heart*, and finally, 4) Process this with someone.

Exercise # 21

Retrain your brain

Addiction is a developmental adaptive condition. It is a condition that started out in your early childhood, therefore your brain has been conditioned neurologically to your acting out behaviors. There are chemicals in the brain involved in the process. The brain's neural networks configure themselves in response to certain environmental experiences. The only way to stop this neurological process is through retraining. This involves a salient method:

1. Desensitize your thoughts of your addictive stimuli by allowing the thoughts to flood your mind (don't resist them) while at the same time not allowing yourself to act out. This way you are training your brain to not connect the thoughts of the addiction to acting out. Acting out behaviors only sends the brain a rush of chemicals and conditions it.

2. When a compulsive thought enters your mind, do not feed the thought by acting on it. This is not to say you ignore the problem. This is an exercise to not feed your brain the neurological responses it is used to. The more you condition your mind to connect yourself with an addictive behavior, the further you will be from recovery. In contrast, the more you train your brain to connect with the non-acting out, the closer you move toward recovery.

Exercise # 22

Identifying and fixing your triggers

What specifically makes you tick? In this exercise you will think about what triggers there are to your addiction. Triggers can be things like free time on Friday nights or driving past a particular bar or store. Whatever your triggers are, come up with strategies to fix them. For example, if a particular adult book store is a trigger then the "fix it" strategy would be to not drive past that store. You will have to drive another route. Much of this involves behavioral techniques, but fixing triggers gives you little leeway to relapse and promotes a good recovery environment.

The Trigger	"To fix it" Strategy
____________________________________	____________
____________________________________	____________
____________________________________	____________
____________________________________	____________
____________________________________	____________
____________________________________	____________
____________________________________	____________
____________________________________	____________
____________________________________	____________
____________________________________	____________
____________________________________	____________
____________________________________	____________

Exercise # 23

Sex/Masturbation inventory

Compulsive masturbation and sexual activity with addictive fantasies is an area many struggle with. Many of my clients complain, "Jim, you don't understand, sex is the only thing I have." As if they will die if they can't have it! However, it is not a necessity like food, clothing, and shelter. But to listen to some of these guys you would think it was. In my opinion, it's all manipulation. It is a way to avoid true recovery; it's a way to avoid the real issues. Compulsive masturbation or sex only fuels the fire and will inhibit recovery. This is not talking about healthy sex in a committed relationship; rather this is about the compulsive activity feeding into an addiction. There is a difference. In this exercise inventory you will monitor behaviors, associate thoughts and feeling processes.

When you have sex/masturbate ask yourself the following:

Inventory	Yes	No
1. Is this a stress release?	___	___
2. Am I trying to avoid or medicate a feeling?	___	___
3. Am I responding to someone I saw, or an image or thought?	___	___
4. Will I want to keep this a secret?	___	___
5. Is this a legitimate way of relating with others?	___	___
6. Am I confused about what I really want?	___	___
7. Would sex in a committed monogamous relationship be better than this?	___	___
8. Do I have to have sex/masturbate when I am horny?	___	___
9. Will I feel guilty or badly afterwards?	___	___
10. Am I afraid my closest friends would not understand this?	___	___

If you have more yes answers then no, sex or masturbation is used to avoid the real issues. You will need to talk to someone about this and develop an action plan ASAP.

Action Plan: ____

____

____

____

____

____

____

Exercise # 24

Practice safe driving

Being in a car alone can be difficult for people in recovery. Being behind the wheel and having the accessibility to drive anywhere can fuel you to take detours. For one, it serves to fulfill conquest desires. Driving by a particular adult book store or bar area can bring a rush of excitement in the body. It's like hunting; search until you capture. For some, it can be a game of attention seeking and pleasure seeking. The problem is that excessive amounts of time are wasted, which never leads to fulfillment of legitimate needs anyways. The underlying issue really is loneliness. In this exercise you are asked to read the following successful tips and practice them to help your driving experience be less of a threat to your recovery.

Tips

- Always have a specific place to drive to. Never go on an open-ended trip.
- Avoid areas that are known for being high risk, e.g. cruise spots, adult book stores, college campuses, main streets, parks, bar strips, prostitute hang outs, drug environments, etc.
- Get yourself an accountability partner and tell that person when you will be on the road and when you will reach your destination. Ask them to call you on your cell phone and check on you.
- Avoid driving alone if at all possible. Remember, one of the recovery traps is isolation.
- Is public transportation safer for you? If so, use it.
- If driving alone is a huge problem for you, in the early stages of recovery have someone drive you or drive with you.
- Avoid listening to those media trap radio stations and music that glorify addictions. Listen to safe music and talk radio or books on tape.
- If you need to talk to someone on your hands-free phone, do so. Again, isolation is not helpful.
- Avoid "pit stops," extended trips, and down times when driving.

Remember, if you fail to plan, you plan to fail!

Exercise # 25

Accountability

In recovery, you must have someone available that you can tell everything to. This person can help you, but only if you let him. You must allow this person to challenge you and he must know how. In this exercise you will identify who will keep you accountable. They must be available, safe and mature and have resolved their own issues. Don't try to be helped by someone who is drowning, you'll both drown! Below are some specific areas in which you will need accountability. Review this list with your accountability partner so that you are on the same page.

Accountability partner	Contact info/phone numbers
______________________	___________________________
Alternate: ______________	___________________________

Key Accountability Areas Checklist:

Internet
Allow someone to monitor your activity; link your activities to their computer for monitoring; give them the passwords.

Money
Is any money going to fuel addictions?
Limit your credit line. Give someone statement account access. Have your credit card company alert them upon usages.

Time
Provide someone your daily schedule/whereabouts.
Discuss down times and have plans.
Someone should be able to challenge you if there is no time made for friendships and activities in recovery.

Business/work
Share with someone your work stress and any conflicts. Don't be proud. and don't hide anything.

Relationships
Someone should be able to help challenge you in your relationships. They should be able to help you process hurts in relationships. They can help you role play through tough problems.

Behaviors
You must be able to discuss all areas of behaviors with someone including histories, slips, and relapses. One suggestion is to share the results of the inventories you complete in this workbook.

Exercise # 26

HALT

H.A.L.T. is an acronym that stands for Hungry, Angry, Lonely, and Tired. It is often used in recovery circles. The items stand for the red flags to acting out. In other words, when you are lonely, you are most vulnerable to a fall. To prevent this, you need an action plan. The action plan can be both proactive/preventive and reactive/curative. The proactive/preventive plan helps you avoid getting lonely. A reactive/curative plan is when it's too late and loneliness has already peaked its evil head. You will then need to know what to do. In this exercise you are asked to set up both a proactive/preventive and a reactive/curative plan using the H.A.L.T. acronym.

I: Proactive/preventive plan. What I will do to avoid the following from taking its toll:

Hungry – ____

Angry – ____

Lonely – ____

Tired – ____

II: Reactive/curative plan. What I will do when the following takes its toll:

Hungry – ____

Angry – ____

Lonely – ____

Tired – ____

Exercise # 27

Disputing negative self-talk

Behavior therapists have a long history of success helping clients change the way they think. This has resulted in people not only feeling better about themselves, but overcome chronic problems such as depression and low self-esteem. Dr. David Burns in his books, *Ten Days to Self-esteem* and the *Feeling Good Handbook* has created several practical exercises to help people. Another good workbook is *Mind over Mood* by Greenberger, D. & Padesky, C. A.

The famous British psychiatrist J.A. Hadfield tested the effects of mental suggestion on the strength of three men measured by a dynamometer. Under different sets of conditions they were asked to grip the dynamometer with all their might:

1. When tested under normal waking conditions their average grip was 101 pounds.
2. When tested under hypnosis and told they were "weak" they could only grip 29 pounds; less than a third their normal strength, and finally,
3. When tested under hypnosis and told they were "strong" they could grip an average of 142 pounds; an increase of almost fifty percent.

This proved that when the mind is filled with positive thoughts of strength one can increase his power by almost 50%.

One client I was working with asked why is it that he sometimes sabotages himself when he is placed in a situation which may result in others seeing him at his best or accepting him. He said, "I have heard on more than one occasion a little voice inside of me that says: 'You're going to blow it' or 'You're not going to be able to do that the right way and he/she/they are going to think you are stupid.' When this happens, I try my best but I usually come close to messing up whatever I'm doing and sometimes I do." So, why do we do this? This "sabotage" he describes is merely a maladaptive cognitive distortion. When it comes to others accepting or embracing him, he put up defenses since he has been let down in the past by those so close to him, especially his dad and male peers. In this example, self-talk can help: "Where it is written that I have to be liked by this guy?" The next time you catch yourself in predicaments such as described, test the evidences: 1) It is probably not the case (in reality), but rather your interpretation against your own favor. 2) If he really does think badly of you, then forget him and the boat he came on. Because if he does think badly of you, then he has his own hang-ups and should not be suited for your time or investment. Always, once that "little [destructive] voice goes off," dispute it.

Assignment

1. Read: Burns, D. (1989). *The feeling good handbook* and Burns, D. (1993). *Ten days to self- esteem.* New York: Quill/HarperCollins; or Greenberger, D. & Padesky, C. A. (1995). *Mind over mood.* New York: Guilford Press.

2. Complete the practical exercises in the reading assignments listed above.

3. Process this with someone and discuss how this relates to recovery.

Exercise # 28

Identifying and destroying the bad habits in thinking

Mental health experts Albert Ellis, Aaron Beck, and David Burns all agree that most of our problems lie in the way we think. In this exercise you will learn about the negative thinking characteristics that have been assigned to different thought processes. This is also something referred to as "stinking thinking." Look over the list with irrational anger as its example, and see which ones you can identify with. Pay attention to the antidotes to these so that it gives you insight for your own living. After such, use the worksheet on the following page to process your own scenarios.

1. ***Overestimation and underestimation.*** Angry individuals tend to overestimate the probability of negative events and underestimate personal and other coping resources (i.e., initial interpretations of the events are biased toward identifying threatening or frustrating events, whereas secondary interpretations underestimate capacities to problem solve and cope). For example, if your boss says he wants to talk to you, you immediately think, "He's going to fire me," and then tell yourself, "I won't be able to handle it." The antidote is learning to engage in accurate estimation, in which you can challenge negative thoughts with more positive and benign information, and give more credit to yourself for your personal and environmental coping resources.
2. ***Misattributions and single explanations.*** Angry individuals tend to jump to highly personalized conclusions and explanations that may not be based on actual facts, and then respond angrily as if these interpretations are true. Often these attributions involve ideas of injustice, intentionality, controllability, and blameworthiness which further elevate anger. For example, if someone cuts you off on the highway, you tell yourself, "He did that just to provoke me," which leads to a higher level of anger than the thought, "He must not be paying attention." The antidote is "multiplicative thinking," in which you entertain a number of possible alternative explanations and attributions, and then assess their truth.
3. ***Polarized conceptualization.*** In making this cognitive error, many individuals code events in black and white concepts (e.g., good-bad, right-wrong, winners-losers). Any evidence that disconfirms the positive end of the spectrum is automatically viewed as extremely negative. For example, if you don't receive an "A" in one of your courses, you tell yourself, "I'm a total failure, and I'll never accomplish anything." The antidote is "continuous thinking," in which you learn to employ qualifying adjectives, adverbs, and phrases that introduce the shades of gray to your world.
4. ***Overgeneralization.*** Angry individuals tend to make broad, sweeping conclusions that go beyond the details of specific events. These conclusions are often reduced to labels that are applied to self, others, events, or time (e.g., *dumb, worthless, always this way,* etc.) and the people respond to the angry meaning of the label, rather than the specifics. The antidote is to become a more discriminating thinker and to focus on the specifics of a given time and place.
5. ***Inflammatory thinking.*** This cognitive distortion appears to have particular relevance to anger, and involves labeling events or people in highly negative, often obscene or nonsensical, terms (e.g., *jerk, creep,, etc.*). Anger increases as you respond to the emotional meaning of the term. The antidote is to define your terms and recode events in realistically negative ways (e.g., use the term "annoying" rather than labeling someone a "jerk").
6. ***Demanding and commanding.*** This occurs when people elevate their preferences and desires to moral dictates and commandments of self and others (i.e., things should, ought to, have to, gotta be certain ways). The antidote is engaging in "preferential thinking," in which you phrase thoughts in terms of preferences and desires, as opposed to absolute necessities.

Worksheet for Exercise # 28

Overestimation and underestimation: ______________________________

Antidote: ______________________________

Misattributions and single explanations: ______________________________

Antidote: ______________________________

Polarized conceptualization: ______________________________

Antidote: ______________________________

Overgeneralization: ______________________________

Antidote: ______________________________

Inflammatory thinking: ______________________________

Antidote: ______________________________

Demanding and commanding: ______________________________

Antidote: ______________________________

Exercise # 29

<u>Identifying and expressing your feelings</u>

Allowing the expression of true feelings or affect is vital to recovery. Many people struggling with addictions generally lock up or cover up their feelings and expressions. If they do express them, they do so in the *false self*. This is not to say they don't have feelings, it's just that they don't have a healthy way to express them. In some cases, they were taught to be the "good little boy or girl" and not reveal feelings, especially robust feelings such as anger or frustration. In recovery you must be able to express your true feelings and your underlying feelings that have been trapped. One way to do this is through processing. The best way to process feelings is through one-on-one therapy with an affect-based therapist or in group experimental therapy or psychodrama. However, this exercise can help create the data you need to process feelings. It is an inventory of what feelings you can easily express and which ones you have a hard time expressing. To help you, please refer to the feelings list found in **Appendix A**. Circle the feelings you have a problem expressing. After this, pick the top 3. List them below and then ask the questions for each feeling that follows.

<u>Top 3</u>

1.____
2.____
3.____

Questions:

What do you know about this feeling?

What have you been told about this feeling?

How do others view this feeling?

What would happen if you expressed this feeling?

How long has it been this way?

How and when would you like to express this feeling? With whom?

Exercise # 30

Improving communication skills

Communication is said to make or break you and there is some truth in that. Proper communication involves speaking what's on your mind in a tactful manner as to get the results you want. Folks struggling with addictions find communication to be a major issue. For many, their current communication is a complete disaster. That is, when they speak their needs, they are not properly communicated. When they need to assert themselves, they don't. Every interpersonal behavior is in fact a communication. Everything done in the presence of another person sends out a message. In this exercise you will learn the steps to effectively communicate your needs.

Follow these steps when trying to deal with a person whom you are struggling to communicate with:

- Ask yourself, "What verbal and non-verbal cues is the person giving me?"

- Then think, "What might this person be trying to communicate to me?" By focusing and attempting to understand the message, you can calm your emotional reaction. Staying calm puts you in control.

- Ask yourself, "What is it that *I* want to come out of this interaction?" Forget power trips, they don't work. Remember, the key is getting what YOU want in the process. That's what is important. Don't worry about egos.

- Ask yourself, "How can *I* communicate my message to the individual?" Both verbally and nonverbally,

- then take action.

Communication is an exchange. Be courteous of the other. Use the check list in **Appendix C** for keeping your communication in balance.

Tip: As Dale Carnegie says, the best way to win people is through their hearts. People get a lot of lip service and that's not what they really want. When you communicate, let them know there's something in it for them too. Let them know how it benefits them. Not only will they listen, they will give you what you want and then some. Don't whine and complain when you talk, use a positive, confident voice.

Exercise # 31

Are you passive, aggressive?

One problem I have found with people struggling in addictions is passive, aggressive behaviors. There is nothing wrong with asserting your anger or holding back when appropriate. The problem is when there are repeated patterns, which usually procure consequences. Usually passive behavior will lead to aggressive behavior. For example, if I don't speak up and tell my boss he is using me too much, then after a while I may resent it and one day blow up. The latter is an act of aggression with consequences. Whereas using the skills of communication and assertiveness could assist in this situation. Take the following inventory to assess passive, aggressiveness. Afterwards, answer the questions so you can process this more.

I: Use the following rating system and circle your choices in each item:

The Passive-Aggressive Inventory©

	(1) Rarely	(2) Sometimes	(3) Frequently	(4) Almost Always
1. I try to control things.	1	2	3	4
2. I feel trapped.	1	2	3	4
3. I find out who is to blame.	1	2	3	4
4. I won't rest until I fix it.	1	2	3	4
5. I feel like running away.	1	2	3	4
6. I act and think slowly.	1	2	3	4
7. I act and think quickly.	1	2	3	4
8. I feel like yelling.	1	2	3	4
9. I feel like crying.	1	2	3	4
10. I want revenge.	1	2	3	4

Grouping A
Total your points for

#2,3,5,6,9_________

Grouping B
Total your points for

#1,4,7,8,10_________

Key:
5-10 in any one group you are in the low range
11-15 in any one group you are in the middle range
16-20 in any one group you are in the high range

Grouping A: Passive
Grouping B: Aggressive

II: Processing questions:
1. Which grouping, passive or aggressive, do you lean more towards?
2. Are these the results that you expected?
3. Having middle or high range in both groups can indicate passive-aggressive traits. If this applies to you, and given the discussion about this, what situations and experiences are unique to you?
4. What are some examples of how your highest grouping has played out in your life?

Exercise # 32

Turning threats into rewards

There are many victories to be won in overcoming addictions. When threats to recovery come along, it is not so much the threat itself that's the problem; rather it is what you do with the threat. The worst thing to do is submit to it. Threats will come along even when you have gotten into the final stages of recovery. In Chinese the symbol for the word *threat* denotes a "moment of danger and of opportunity". The following exercise will help you to cope with threats so that you come out a winner.

I: Expose the threat:

Whenever you are threatened, no matter what it is, answer the following questions:

1. What is it that is really threatening me?
2. What will this do to me?
3. What is the worst that can happen?

Doing this will help you to isolate what it is that is really threatening you. This will help you set the foundation for action.

II: Identify the opportunities or rewards:

In every situation ask what are your possibilities and opportunities:

- for becoming wiser and stronger?
- for becoming more loving?
- for growing and learning?
- for gains and benefits?

III: Action plan:

1. How will I use this threat toward an opportunity?
2. What do I have to lose and what do I have to gain? Weigh it and take the best course of action.
3. How will I use the opportunity to grow and change?

Exercise # 33

How do you describe yourself?

Have you really thought about how you describe yourself? Getting in touch with how you really see yourself is helpful in the recovery process. If you had to think of ten words to describe yourself, what would they be?

Use the spaces below or use your notebook to write ten words that you feel describe yourself. Be honest.

1.______________________	6.______________________
2.______________________	7.______________________
3.______________________	8.______________________
4.______________________	9.______________________
5.______________________	10.______________________

Which ones do you consider negative? Why?

Which ones are positive? Why?

Is this what you feel others would say about you?

If not, what would be the difference?

What would you like to change and what could be an action plan?

Exercise # 34

Pick their brain

List three or more people you know who have had a problem with any type of addiction and have been helped. If you don't know of anyone personally, ask someone for referrals.

Go to at least three of these people and, after explaining your situation, ask them for their advice or assistance. Pay attention to any skills they mention that they have used to ameliorate their problems. Record their responses.

What was instrumental to their recovery?

What are their strengths?

What are their weaknesses?

How has this exercise influenced your thinking about addiction and how it can be solved?

Don't forget to process this with someone!

Exercise # 35

Writing an unfinished business letter

Writing about unfinished or even untapped business will bring things to the surface. With this new found data you can learn to not only examine it, but learn to express the feelings that accompany it. In this exercise, complete the following and then process it with someone:

Write a factual account of the situation that has lead up to your addiction:

What haven't you said that you might need to say now?

Explain your feelings about this:

Is there anything else you want to include in the letter? Anything else you need to say that no one else has heard?

What do you want to do with the letter?

List three things that you could do with the letter that might be meaningful to you?

Exercise # 36

Surviving the riptides

Ever wonder what's holding you back? Ever feel like you were in a riptide? You may be surprised at what it is that is really pushing you further away from your recovery. In the following exercise you will be challenged to think about this.

- What forces are pushing you out to sea? That is, what is blocking you from achieving your goals? Be specific; name them.
- If you were to face these forces head on, what would happen? What's at risk for either getting what you want or stopping self-defeating behaviors?
- If you have tried something in the past, what did you do and what happened?
- If you were to do nothing, what would happen?
- What can you do to push back to shore? Meaning, what specific steps will you take to get what you need. Be specific – make simple, measurable goals.

Exercise # 37

Role reversal

Addiction is a serious issue and should not be taken lightly. However, sometimes the struggler uses their addiction as a crutch, or an excuse to act out or to be a certain way. This has to change. In this exercise you will challenge yourself to get out of this rut.

- ✓ Using a notebook, list five occasions where your addictions typically influence your other behaviors or attitudes.
- ✓ Imagine you don't have the problem. List at least seven specific things you would do differently in your everyday life.
- ✓ Now act out a new behavior as though you don't have an addiction.
- ✓ What does this look like? Draw pictures if that helps.
- ✓ What are the results of this new behavior?

Exercise # 38

Dialoguing with your addiction

Dialoguing with your addiction; now that sounds strange! While it does sound strange, it has a powerful effect. It allows you to see the problem from both a subjective and objective view. This exercise will allow you to express how you really feel about addiction.

On a separate piece of paper, write a letter to your addiction. This could include:

- Your feelings about it
- How you see it
- What you want from it
- The consequences of it
- Anything else

✓ Next, be the addiction and write a response to the issues you raise about it.

✓ Then, write another letter to it in response to what it told you.

✓ How was the second and third letter different from the first?

✓ What did you learn from this exercise?

Exercise # 39

Map for the future

No one can really predict the future; however you can plan for the future as best as possible. One way to do so is to have some goals, even if they are not detailed. This exercise will help you start to think about your future and get clear on what you would like to see happen in your life:

I: List three possible options you'd like to see before you.

1. ______________________________

2. ______________________________

3. ______________________________

II: Imagine yourself five years from now having taken on one of the options. Now let your imagination go and answer the following questions:

1. Where do you live and how do you feel about it?

____

____

2. How do you spend your time and how do you feel about it?

____

____

3. Describe your relationship with key people in your life:

____

____

Exercise # 40

<u>Getting your needs met</u>

We have both physical and emotional needs as well as spiritual needs. In this exercise you will process what your needs are, what keeps you from doing what is necessary to get them met, and what you *can* do to get them met.

1. What do you need and deserve?

Physical needs: <u>Ex. I need to be held.</u>

Emotional needs: ____________________

Spiritual needs: ____________________

2. What might keep you from doing that which is necessary to get your needs met?

Physical needs: <u>Ex. I am afraid it will turn sexual</u>

Emotional needs: ____________________

Spiritual needs: ____________________

3. What you <u>can</u> do to get your needs met?

Physical needs: <u>Ex. Ask someone to hold me; someone who won't let me sexualize the situation.</u>

Emotional needs: ____________________

____

Spiritual needs: ____________________

____

Exercise # 41

Check out your response system

How do you respond to stimuli? Believe it or not, your response is not a monolithic approach but rather it is a full systems approach. The system encompasses your physical, emotional, and behavioral symptoms. In this exercise use the checklist below and check off the symptoms you get when you are tested to the limit. Once you identify your symptoms, develop a plan to address them.

STRESS RESPONSE INDEX
0 = This symptom rarely or never occurs.
1 = This symptom occurs occasionally.
2 = This symptom occurs quite often.
3 = This symptom occurs all the time or nearly all the time.

Physiological Symptoms
____ racing or pounding heart
____ rapid breathing with short, shallow breaths
____ cold sweaty palms
____ excessive perspiration
____ asthma attack
____ butterflies in stomach
____ nausea
____ constipation
____ diarrhea
____ dry mouth
____ high blood pressure
____ sudden and urgent need to urinate
____ tics or twitching muscles
____ heartburn/indigestion
____ stomach cramps or pains
____ tremors or shakiness
____ headaches
____ back pain
____ change in appetite
____ impaired sexual function
____ chronic fatigue, exhaustion
____ frequent urination
____ arthritis pain
____ weight change
____ itching
____ dry skin
____ allergy flare-up
____ colds or the flu
____ skin rash
____ other; specify ______________

Emotional Symptoms
____ difficulty concentrating
____ feelings of being sad, blue, or down in the dumps
____ feelings of anxiety, panic, or being out of control
____ forgetfulness
____ suspiciousness
____ racing thoughts

Exercise # 41, continued

____ recurring thoughts you cannot get rid of
____ inability to enjoy the things you used to enjoy
____ feeling as if you will explode
____ restlessness
____ diminished ability to daydream or fantasize
____ mood swings
____ decreased interest in sex
____ decreased interest in previously enjoyed foods
____ being withdrawn, socially isolated
____ apathy
____ cynicism
____ other; specify _______________

Behaviors
____ erratic work habits
____ increased use of sick time
____ excessive worrying
____ excessive use of alcohol or other drugs
____ excessive accidents or injuries
____ overeating
____ excessive complaints
____ increased craving for tobacco or sweets
____ change in sleep patterns (difficulty falling asleep/waking up more frequently during the night)
____ angry outbursts
____ nightmares
____ lack of punctuality for work and/or other important functions
____ gritting teeth
____ nail biting
____ finger or foot tapping
____ other; specify _______________

Action Plan

1. Practice exercise # 48….. ____
2. ____
3. ____
4. ____
5. ____
6. ____
7. ____
8. ____
9. ____
10. ____
11. ____
12. ____
13. ____
14. ____
15. ____

Exercise # 42

Moving from unrealistic expectations to realistic expectations

In our visions we sometimes have unrealistic expectations of ourselves and others. This can be a trap toward self-defeating feelings. In this exercise you will start to look at expectations in a different way. In the worksheet below, isolate those expectations that may be unrealistic in one column. Then process the subsequent columns to get to a resulting feeling that puts you in a win-win situation:

Unrealistic expectations

Ex. "I will not be free from this frustration and defeat..."

Underlying hope

"To be happy; secure"

Resulting feelings

"Sadness when I am defeated."

Realistic expectation

"I will be able to get up again. I may not be totally freed now, but I can have victories each day."

Resulting feeling

"Satisfaction, relief."

Exercise # 43

Let the feelings flow

Feelings should be processed, not ignored or covered up. You must confront strong feelings openly. If you don't allow feelings to be expressed, they will only leak out in physical, emotional, or mental symptoms. Use the five steps listed below as a guide to processing your feelings. Refer to **Appendix A** for an example of the various types of feelings.

Steps to Letting Go

If you confront guilt, anger, and other strong feelings openly, whatever emotional leftovers you have not mourned *can* be let go. Use these five steps as a guide:

1. ***Recognize the feeling.*** When a feeling emerges, don't push it away. Instead, stay with it, taking time to identify it. Close your eyes and experience it. Locate the feeling in your body. Can you attach a color or an image to it? Give the feeling a name: for example, *sadness*.
2. ***Express the feeling.*** Say aloud, to yourself or another person, "I am feeling sad about _________."
3. ***Clarify the feeling.*** Examine the feeling further to see what's behind it. In the case of sadness, you are probably mourning the ending of something that began with joy and hope, or you may find you are also angry at someone for leaving or dying, thus destroying your dream of a relationship. You may feel guilty for having left or for being the one left alive. Clarify what the feeling really is all about, it's many components: "I'm sad, mad, and afraid. And I feel guilty, too."
4. ***Explain the feeling.*** As you go deeper into the feeling, you might find another reason at the core of it. Sadness about your ended relationship may have concealed anger at someone leaving, anger that, when recognized, may in turn have exposed deeply rooted fears of abandonment or rejections. When you can identify and explain the feeling's source, you can begin to respond with new behavior. At this point, you may even want to rename the feeling. Beneath what you once labeled sorrow, for example, may be a deep fear that can be traced to your childhood: "I felt the same way when I was a child and watched Dad and Mom fight."
5. ***Accept the feeling.*** Feelings are neither good nor bad; they just are. You are not a "good" or "bad" person because you have these feelings. None of us has constant control over what we feel from minute to minute. Realize that you're human, like everyone else in the world! When you stop judging feelings "good" or "bad," you can learn to accept them. Having accepted your own, you will find it easier to accept the feelings of others as well.

Exercise # 44

<u>Try new activities often</u>

Being in a rut, doing the same things over and over, or idle times are not conductive to recovery. In order to move past this, it is important to try new activities. By being versatile, you put yourself in places to meet new people and form new relationships. This is why activities are so important. In this exercise review the list of activity suggestions found in **Appendix B** and choose some to do each week. The list is not exclusive; it is just for suggestions. Try to do activities that involve others. Mix it up so that you try new and different things each week.

See Inventory in Appendix B

Exercise # 45

Monitoring your anger response

This exercise is to help you increase your awareness of situations in which you become angry. Remember, anger is a natural feeling. Do not ignore it. Try to understand it and its roots. By doing this you will be able to properly address your anger and work it out in a therapeutic manner. Use the monitoring response form below. After such, process the results with someone. You may want to proceed to Exercise # 46, *Interpreting anger* after completing this exercise.

Monitoring Response Form

Activating event or incident	Anger 0-10*	Physical Response	Thoughts/Behaviors
(Example) Some guy at the gym took my bench when I went for a drink of water	*7*	*Muscle tension* *Clenched jaws* *Headache*	*Behavior: I snapped at him.* *Thoughts: Who the heck does he think he is. How dare he take my bench.*

* Scale: Anger 1-10. 10 is the worst, 0 is none at all.

Exercise # 46

<u>Interpreting anger</u>

Now that you have learned to monitor your anger, it is time to process it and do something constructive and therapeutic with it so that it is not displaced and holds you down. In this exercise you can draw on those incidents that have caused a particular thought/behavior. This time, however, you will have to parallel another time when you felt that way and discuss the particulars. Note any new feeling this may bring. See if you can find a connection? Finally, think up a strategy that will be a healthy way to address this feeling.

Processing Anger Worksheet

Incident	Thoughts/Behaviors Strategy	What other time have I felt like this	New affect	Action
(ex. Some guy took my bench at the gym).	*I snapped at him. Who the heck does he think he is. How dare he take my bench?*	*I used to feel this way when my brother would take my stuff from me.*	*Pissed off*	*I will hit a bag* *Or* *Talk to the guy*

Exercise # 47

What can I do about my anger?

1. **Apply Step One.** "We admitted we were powerless over our anger and that our lives had become unmanageable." By admitting we are powerless to control what, where, and when we feel angry, we deepen our awareness of the very nature of feeling. We have no more control over any feeling than we do over thoughts that pop in and out of our minds.

2. Remember that anger is a feeling. Everyone feels it. Anger is natural, healthy, non-evil, and human.

3. Feeling anger and acting out anger are not the same thing. Therefore, I am responsible for what I do.

4. **My anger is my own.** The other person did not "make" me angry.

5. **Get to know your anger triggers.** "Find your own buttons, so you'll know when they're pushed."

6. **Don't set yourself up to get angry.** If your temperature rises when you are waiting in a slow line at the supermarket, shop at a less busy time of day. Work at finding resolutions.

7. **Talk about your feelings.** Friends, sponsors, other group members, and family can often support **you** and your feelings. Do not use them to make yourself "right."

8. **Avoid justifying your anger.** Remember, self-righteous anger is a killer.

9. **State your feelings directly,** with appropriate non-verbal cues. For example: *"I feel angry when you..."* If you are genuinely angry, a smile is inappropriate.

10. **Develop coping strategies** to deal with the discomfort of anger. For example: Relaxation, physical exercise, breathing, taking "time outs," affirmations.

11. **Practice assertively expressing your anger.** Avoid name-calling, put-downs, one-upmanship.

12. **Pray.** The Serenity Prayer helps with both external and internal resolution.

13. **Deal with issues as they arise.** Avoid stewing about an issue for hours, days, or weeks. If you are unable to address the conflict immediately, arrange a specific time when you can and will.

14. **Work toward resolution.** Resolution of the conflict, resolution of the feeling.

Exercise # 48

Cue-controlled relaxation

Relaxation will not take away addictions, but it will take away the stress related to the battles you face each day. It will help you to be more in control and in that sense will help you in the recovery process. The following is a procedure you can use:

What is it?

Although it is important to master longer, deeper relaxation techniques, it is also important to learn techniques to practice during the day, regardless of where you are. After all, that's where we usually feel most tense! Cue-controlled relaxation involves identifying a cue, or reminder, for ourselves and practicing a simple "letting go" relaxation technique whenever and wherever we see or hear the cue. Cues can be based on time (every 90 minutes) or event (whenever I hear a phone ring); they can be visual (like leaving notes to yourself) or internal (whenever I notice my heart rate increasing). There is no limit to the type of cues you might choose to utilize – the important thing is that you select a cue and practice this simple relaxation technique every time you encounter the cue.

Why?

Once you have mastered the more in-depth techniques, cue-controlled relaxation gives you a fast way to become relaxed. It also helps you to retrain yourself in anger-provoking settings (work, freeway, social situations). The ultimate goal of stress management is to develop new habits in daily activities.

How to do it:

1. Take a deep breath.
2. Exhale slowly.
3. Say "relax" (or some other word e.g., "calm," "peace," "one," etc.) to yourself as you exhale.
4. If possible, also close your eyes for a few seconds and concentrate on letting your muscles become less tense.

IMPORTANT

IT IS ESSENTIAL THAT YOU RESPOND EACH AND EVERY TIME YOU ENCOUNTER THE CUE. FOCUS YOUR ENTIRE ATTENTION ON DOING THE PROCEDURE, NOT ON WHETHER YOU THINK YOU HAVE ENOUGH TIME OR WHETHER YOU THINK IT WILL BE "EFFECTIVE."

Exercise # 49

Photo analysis

Family photographs can help you gather and process information about family dynamics. In this exercise you will examine family of origin photos and analyze the dynamics and process the current feelings associated to the photos.

I: Pick out 10 -15 photos from family of origin photo albums. Try to go back as early in childhood as possible for some. Some can be more recent. You do not necessarily have to be in every photo. Try, however to find most that include yourself interacting with others.

II: Complete the following questions to help you in this processing exercise:

1. Did the photo call you visually, or was your response more from your body or your gut (feelings)?

2. Look at each photo separately. For each, consider the thoughts, emotions, memories, and fantasies that you become aware of while looking at the photo. How does each photo make you feel? What do you think about when viewing it?

3. What does each photo mean? What message does it send? Does is say anything to you now?

4. If you could travel back in time to the shooting of the photo, what would you change?

5. Pretend you could cut one person or thing out of the picture. What or who would you choose? Explain.

6. What story can you tell about this photo?

For more work in photo therapy, a suggested reading is:

Weiser, J. (1993). *Phototherapy techniques: Exploring the secrets of personal snapshots and family albums.* San Francisco: Jossey-Bass.

Exercise # 50

Questioning the acting out motives

In recovery you will have acting out motives. Be aware! One way to challenge the motives is to ask yourself what is going on. Beyond that, it means getting help. Don't forgo this yourself, get help.

Questions:

When you start to move toward acting out, stop and ask yourself:

What is it that I am really trying to get out of this?

What red flags are going up?

What lies am I listening to now?

How many days have I been planning this?

What event or events are coming up?

Who have I been avoiding?

What tools am I not using?

Have I been feeling less powerful over the problem lately?

Is there a reward in this?

Am I testing anything?

Am I being honest in my plan of recovery?

Exercise # 51

What my addiction took and takes from me

Addiction comes with a cost. In this exercise you are challenged to think about the many things it took from you and may still be taking from you. In addictions, much has been stolen. Examples include broken marriages, health, finances, emotional wellness, and so on. In the spaces below or in a notebook, list the losses that it dealt you and perhaps is still dealing you.

1. ______________________________

2. ______________________________

3. ______________________________

4. ______________________________

5. ______________________________

6. ______________________________

7. ______________________________

8. ______________________________

9. ______________________________

10. ______________________________

Exercise # 52

Picture this

Draw two pictures: One with yourself in your addiction and one without. Compare and contrast. Process this with someone or in group.

With:

Without:

Exercise # 53

Understanding your childhood roles

I: Review the common roles children assume in dysfunctional families:

Lost Child
- The one who is overlooked
- The one who seems unwanted
- He will try to balance the family by not causing any problems or rocking the boat.

Surrogate Spouse
- The child who is forced to be the emotional caregiver of a parent due to the parent's lack of confidence in her partner or absence of partner; also referred to as "emotional incest"

Little Parent
- If the parent of a child is dysfunctional, the child rises to the occasion to take on the parenting role to siblings or even to the parent(s)
- An example is a case where a brother takes on the "little parent" role to help his brother since the father had abandoned them

Hero
- A child becomes an overachiever to give the shame-based family a sense of dignity
- Tries to be perfect; "save the world"

The Protected One
- The one everyone tries to shield
- Shipped off to others or other systems; e.g. an affluent boy who is shipped to boarding school really because the mother is an alcoholic and the father wants to "protect" him
- This person becomes isolated; in the dark
- No one explains anything is wrong, tells him everything is alright

Scapegoat
- When intensity reaches, this person, usually the most sensitive, becomes the blame
- The function of the role is to absorb the shame so to lessen the responsibility of the others

Clown
- Laugh of the party. Acts up to get attention.

II: Processing Questions:

1. Which role(s) did you mostly identify with growing up?
2. How does this affect you today?
3. If none of the roles above fit you, describe your unique role:

Exercise # 54

My relationship with my father

Describe your relationship with your dad:

(Note: If you had a stepfather, do this for your stepfather. If you had more than one, do one for each. Use a notebook to add more description.)

As a child:____

As a teenager:____

As an adult:____

Feelings:

What negative feelings do I have towards my dad?____________________________

What positive feelings do I have towards my dad?____________________________

I wish my dad…(finish this. It can be more than one sentence if you like):_________

Exercise # 55

My relationship with my mother

Describe your relationship with your mother:

(Note: If you had a stepmother, do this for your stepmother. If you had more than one, do one for each. Use a notebook to add more description.)

As a child:____

____

____

As a teenager:____

____

____

As an adult:____

____

____

Feelings:

What negative feelings do I have towards her?______________________________

____

____

What positive feelings do I have towards her?______________________________

____

____

I wish my mother… (finish this. It can be more than one sentence if you like):______

____

____

Exercise # 56

<u>My relationship with my brother</u>

Describe your relationship with your brother:

(Note: If you had a stepbrother, do this for your stepbrother. If you had more than one brother or stepbrother, do one for each. Use a notebook to add more description.)

As a child:____

As a teenager:____

As an adult:____

<u>Feelings</u>:

What negative feelings do I have towards him?________________________________

What positive feelings do I have towards him?________________________________

I wish my brother… (finish this. It can be more than one sentence if you like):______

Exercise # 57

<u>My relationship with my sister</u>

Describe your relationship with your sister:

(Note: If you had a stepsister, do this for your stepsister. If you had more then one sister or stepsister, do one for each. Use a notebook to add more description.)

As a child:____

____

____

As a teenager:____

____

____

As an adult:____

____

____

<u>Feelings</u>:

What negative feelings do I have towards her?______________________________

____

____

What positive feelings do I have towards her?______________________________

____

____

I wish my sister… (finish this. It can be more than one sentence if you like):________

____

____

Exercise # 58

Control

What do you have control over and what don't you? In this exercise you will be challenged to think about those things you can control and those you can't.

1. Write five or more things about your problem situation that you can control.
   1.____
   2.____
   3.____
   4.____
   5.____

2. How do you control each of these things?
   1.____
   2.____
   3.____
   4.____

3. Write below five or more things about your problem situation that you cannot control.
   1.____
   2.____
   3.____
   4.____
   5.____

4. In what ways have you tried to control these things and what has been your degree of success?
   1.____
   2.____
   3.____
   4.____

Exercise # 59

Forgiving others

At what point do you forgive someone? Inevitably, anyone struggling with addictions has hurt. When do you forgive and how? You may be struggling and asking, "Is it okay not to forgive?" The important thing to keep in mind is that the act of forgiveness releases any burden on your part; it does not necessarily excuse any wrongdoings. For those who are spiritual, forgiveness is a requirement in the brotherhood. In such terms, forgiveness is that you simply write off any debt you feel is owed to you. You can tell the person what they owe you (getting it off your mind), but not necessarily expecting them to pay, as in many cases they could not pay back for all the pain they caused anyway. In this exercise you be able to process thoughts on forgiveness.

What do you feel you deserve that would even the score from someone that hurt you?

What price do you pay for holding this debt?

Have you let the other person know what you think they deserve?

If not, could you?

Can the other person give you what you want?

How can you release the burden of the debt, if the person cannot give you what you want?

Exercise # 60

No more "poor me's"

Psychologist Dr. Gerard J. M. van den Aardweg makes the point that the problem of many maladaptive behaviors is based in infantile childish complaining. The poor me's, feeling like a victim, and self pity are the struggler's doom. In this exercise you will test his theory by not loathing in any self pity. So, keep a log of any self pity parties you have and then make an action plan. As an example, the next time you seek comfort in self pity, a practical exercise plan would have you volunteer for a charity instead. Use the log below and create your own practical action plan:

Area of complaint/self-pity:__Ex:_1. "I am mad that no one appreciates me!"_______

____

____

____

____

____

____

____

Action Plan:

________1. "I will volunteer at a soup kitchen where I am appreciated"___________

____

____

____

Exercise # 61

Know thyself

Once you acquire self-insight then you can change. The best strategy is to pay close attention to what others remark about you. It's like playing an investigator. Look and listen and do not get defensive. All this data is constructive.

Log:

- ✓ Pay close attention to remarks and responses from others about you.
- ✓ Collect the data and make notes.
- ✓ Review this with someone and process it.

Ask yourself:

1. What did I learn?
2. What areas can I change?

Exercise # 62

Keep a diary/journal

Summarizing your daily activities can be very helpful. This process serves to help you unload what's going on each day and provides you an avenue of review so you can see what patterns and trends you are facing. Obtain something you can write in and which you can keep in a safe place. Process your diary or journal with someone periodically. Be honest in your diary or journal Don't just log in activities, log in your thoughts and feelings as well.

Exercise # 63

Fighting self-pity with humor (hyperdramatization)

Dr. Gerard J. M. van den Aardweg helps people to get out of the trap of self pity by using a technique he prescribes as *hyperdramatization.* In practice of this technique, you actually talk to yourself as if you are one's "child." In the example below, he uses the technique of *hyperdramatization* in addressing rejection:

"Poor Johnny, how harshly you've been treated! Beaten up, all bloody, with your clothes torn…" When feeling hurt childish pride, one might say, "You poor thing, your statue in a majestic pose, quite like a little Napoleon, has been hauled down like Lenin's after the fall of communism," while imagining the jeering mob and one's poor "child" coming down, in ropes, crying. To self-pity over loneliness – a highly frequent complaint – one might respond, "Such agony! Your shirt is wet, even the windows are steamed by your tears, and the sheets of your bed are dripping, saturated with your tears; a pond of tears is forming on the floor; fishes with an intensely sad look are swimming aimless circles in it;" and so on.
(P. 117)

Now it's your turn. Identify a time when you felt rejected, lonely, slighted, not accepted, etc. then develop your own hyperdramatization. Be as humorous as possible. You know you get it when you start to laugh and see that you really are using self-pity as a way to deal with normal life variants and that it is ridiculous how you beat yourself up.

Exercise # 64

Assessing the now and then

Between now and your next session, make a list of the things you would like to change. Be specific; list particulars such as experiences or events. Focus on what you do or experience in the situation. Use a notebook or separate pages to log your responses.

1. What will happen if you don't make those changes?
2. When you are finished with counseling or mentoring, what will be different?
3. What will be (or has been) the first and smallest sign that change is beginning?
4. When you notice that first change, what can you do to keep the ball rolling?

Exercise # 65

Healing shame

In this exercise you will learn about shame. Uncovering shame can bring forth your healing. According to Fossum & Mason (1986) "…shame refers to humiliation so painful, embarrassment so deep, and a sense of being so completely diminished that one feels [he] will disappear into a pile of ashes. Shame involves the entire self and self worth of a human being." In essence, shame becomes you. Shame is the self concept that one is bad, inadequate, and worthy of rejection. It becomes a total sense of identity.

According to the authors, there is a correlation between shame and dependency in families entangled in rigid, perfectionist rules. In addition, there is a great deal of blame and denial. This holds true for both enmeshed families (tightly intertwined with no boundaries) and disengaged families (loosely intertwined, with ambiguous boundaries). Hence the term, "shame bound families" is used. My family system for example, was disengaged. Everyone lived in their own little bubble and kept their own little secrets. According to Dr Carl Whitaker, it is delusional to think we have no imperfections. The problem in shame-bound families is that members are taught to look good on the outside and not share what's on the inside. Therefore, a double jeopardy occurs, leading into not being able to feel or express healthy shame. Healthy shame is exposing your wounds and sharing with others what really bothers you, what's really on you mind.

Checklist for healthy shame:
___It is the permission to be human
___Willingness to accept help/feedback
___Love and acceptance of self
___To have a feeling and be able to freely express it without violation

In shame-bound families, members are taught not to expose family secrets, to put on a happy face, even in times of sadness and unrest.

Checklist for roots of shame:
___Abuse, abandonment; whether real or perceived
___Personal violations
___Seductions; can be physical or emotional (e.g. emotional incest).
___Anything that has caused a boundary violation

According to Bradshaw (1987) abuse is not always concrete or overt like physical or sexual abuse. Other variations include: lying to a child, suppressing a child's vital spontaneity, manipulations, scare tactics, withdrawal of love or affection, differential

Exercise # 65, Continued

preferences, fantasy bonding, isolating, coercion, stroke deprivation, child told they are cause of problems, and boundary violations.

Some people tend to confuse shame and guilt. There is a distinction, however, between the two. Guilt is the developmental, more mature, though painful, feeling of regret one has about behavior that has violated a personal value. It does not directly reflect upon one's identity, nor diminish one's self worth. Shame, on the other hand, is the painful feeling about one's self as a person. This is a significant difference. It's healthy to feel bad about committing a violation, it's not healthy when you feel your own identity is shamed and your whole sense of self-worth is diminished. It is not healthy to think you cannot fail; rather it is healthy to talk about your failures and expose your wounds, therefore establishing a supportive community. It is good for others to know about the good, the bad, and the ugly. If you feel you have to be perfect, you then put on a persona, a mask, a false self. Thus, the latter is what the authors find as the "shame-bound" person.

People who struggle in addictions find shame as a core issue. Shame is initiated by the systems they grew up in; that is, family, peers, churches, schools, community, etc. For example, one of my clients had parents who told him he must be the "good boy" at school. As a result, he perceived he was not allowed to have any problems surface. Unknown to his parents, he was picked on at school. One student even made a horrible web page about him. These systems perpetuated his shame. On one hand, he was supposed to be "good" and not complain, but on the other hand, he was perceived as bad by his classmates. He didn't want to disappoint his parents so he kept quiet about the incidents at school. The child with healthy shame would have been able to go to his parent(s) and vent the problems he had at school. However, there is the notion that he shouldn't have problems; hence he failed to bring it to his parent's attention. Because of this, he was robbed the supportive environment needed to help cope with the problems at school.

- To be shame-based is to be intolerable to pain - pain is horrible - so there is always a great need to relieve the pain.

- Relief patterns can consist of a variety of things such as overeating, sexual acting out (e.g. compulsive masturbation, endless hours of fantasy, porn surfing, etc.)

In what ways were you shamed?______________________________________

How has shame affected you?______________________________________

What are some ways to come out of your shame? __________________________

Action plan: ____

Exercise # 66

Understanding narcissism

Alice Miller (1996) theorizes that we all need "basic narcissistic supplies" in order to grow and mature. In other words, children need mirroring from their parents and to be admired and taken seriously.

Some parents crave their own narcissistic needs in their children. This process however injures the child. While the child is there for the parent, they are robbed of their own needs. Because the child is there for the parent, there is no one there to mirror the child's feelings, drives, and the nurturance the child needs. (Referred to also as the *narcissistic wound*).

Consequence: If one is deprived of their narcissistic mirroring, they will seek it in other objects (*object relations* theory). This object can be things like drinking and sexual deviations. These provide their "grandiosity" and mirroring those aspects lost earlier in childhood.

This is an empty path, however, because for the narcissistically wounded, their drug is grandiosity. When that is gone, they feel empty.

Some key points to keep in mind:

- Children need "basic narcissistic supplies." That is, mirroring and the need to be admired.
- It injures a child when a parent(s) robs them of this need.
- If one is deprived of basic narcissistic needs, then they will seek it in other objects (*Object Relations*). Object Relations can be things like drinking, sexing, stealing, all of which can provide the grandiosity and mirroring aspects lost in early development.

Processing questions:

1. How have you been robbed of your healthy narcissistic needs?

2. In what ways have you had to get narcissistic needs met?

3. Proceed to do inner child work (Exercise # 18) to help bring out healthy narcissistic needs.

Exercise # 67

Understanding denial and other defense mechanisms

Being in true recovery means we don't need to lie to ourselves or others any longer. Denial is our escape from reality, our fantasy. It's lying to ourselves. It the false belief that all is fine and that we are in control. Denial keeps us from the truth. Many of us feel that our addiction has its own personality and voice. We all have different parts or aspects to our personality. For example, most of us feel and behave differently at work than when we are with our parents, around our kids, on a date, or in a classroom. We tell our kids not to lie and mean it, but we then lie to our boss, the IRS, and our friends. It is as if we have different and real personalities existing in our consciousness. The addiction also has a life of its own and its own voice. To stay "alive," it creates its own story to tell us. Essentially, it tells us we are fine and do not have the problem so we can keep us in it. This untrue story that we hear is our denial.

To recover from any addiction we need to know how our disease lies to us and how we lie to ourselves. We bring the truth in so we can have a chance to change our broken lives. Denial is a protective mechanism; it is a defense. It keeps us from feeling the painful and uncomfortable truth about both our powerlessness and the consequences or unmanageability of our addictions. If we cannot feel or see these consequences, everything is fine and our disease can stay alive and active. We have denial to protect us from pain.

To recover, we need to see our denial and see how it works so that we can loosen the grip of our addictions. Denial is replaced by the truth and acceptance. To be in denial feels like anger, fear, shame, and isolation. Instead of being cold and cut off from ourselves and others, we can be warm and begin to grow again.

Defenses are the specific way we ward off attacks to our denial. Some defenses are conscious and we are aware of them. Others are subconscious. We use both to keep our denial intact.

Review the list below of common defenses, or forms of denial.

1. **Simple denial** – Simply denying being addicted. Example: *"You're an alcoholic." "No, I'm not."*
2. **Minimizing** – This is about making our chemical dependency or using seem less than it is . Example: *"Yes, I drink, but not that much." "I wasn't that bad at the party."*
3. **Rationalizing** – Making excuses about or for the behaviors. Examples: *"I can't sleep, so I drink or take pills." "I need narcotics for my bad back." "I had a bad day." "A man needs a little sex on the side sometimes."*

Exercise # 67, Continued

4. **Blaming** – Using because we "had to." Something "made us." The responsibility lies somewhere else, not with us. Example: *"If my wife was nicer, I wouldn't need to____!" "I lost my job, that's what made me____."*

5. **Bargaining** – Cutting deals. Example: *"I'll quit if you quit smoking." "I'll quit when there's less stress at work."*

6. **Intellectualizing or Generalizing** – Using theories about the addiction, keeping it general and vague. Example: *"My family is alcoholic and I have the wrong genes." "My childhood was so bad, it's a way of coping with my underlying feelings."*

7. **Diversion** – Changing the subject. Example: *"Yeah I got drunk last night, so what's for dinner?"* or *"My sexing bothers you? Your weight bothers me!"*

8. **Passivity** - Ignoring it or being a victim. Example: *"I've tried to quit, but it's stronger than me." "There's nothing I can do." "If I only had more willpower..."*

9. **Hostility** – Scaring or threatening people away from discussing it. Example: *"I'm lousy in bed when I'm drunk? Fine, no more sex." "Get off my back!" "You like my paychecks, don't you?"*

<u>When primary defense fails, secondary defenses are often used:</u>

Inhibition: You become paralyzed when you want to do something (e.g. you want to call someone but you can't).
Reaction formation: You keep all shame triggers out of conscious. To be cruel would induce shame, so you act kind.
Undoing: Magical behaviors (e.g. rituals) are used to cancel out feelings that will cause shame.
Isolation of affect: Use of one thought, for example, "I want to have sex…" to distract from the real painful experience.
Turning against self: Self abuse (e.g. head banging, cutting, ritualistic masturbations).
The false self: Once internalized, you no longer have the feeling of shame – you are it. Because you see yourself as flawed and defective, you cannot look at yourself without pain. Therefore, you create a false self. "The False Self" is what Jungians call the *persona* (the mask) and Transactional-Analysis (TA) call the *adapted child.* The false self is always hiding, filled with secrets; never giving full self-disclosure, making bad parts seems good and hiding vulnerabilities.

Exercise # 67, Continued

Characterological styles of defense:

Perfectionism: For example, "I am valued by doing."
Striving for power and control: This defense is used by controlling others; power is seen as the control; it makes you feel powerful to control others, but really it is a false self.
Rage: A cover up, keeps others away, transfer shame to others, and protects the self against further experiences.

Defenses can be interpersonally transferred:

- Through arrogance, criticism (e.g. "If I feel put down I can reduce the feeling by criticizing others"), blame, judgment, and contempt (reject the other)
- By being nice – Avoids real emotional contact; phony, unreal, and really puts limits on the relationship
- Through compulsive behaviors and reenactments – Being shame-based is to be in intolerable pain – pain is horrible – so there is great need to relieve the pain. You feel you need something outside of yourself to take away your terrible feelings.
  Relief patterns can consist of overeating, sexual acting out (e.g. masturbation and fantasy, porn surfing), drugging, etc.

Processing Questions:

1. What defense mechanism(s) can you identify with? Why?
2. How has this taken its toll in your life?
3. Now that this is conscious, what plans can you make to overcome these defenses?

Exercise # 67a.

Looking at the denial around my addiction

In this exercise list under each dynamic an example of how this has played out in your addiction. Then process this toward finding a way to challenge a behavior that is contrary to that denial pattern.

1. **Simple denial**

2. **Minimizing**

3. **Rationalizing**

4. **Blaming**

5. **Bargaining**

6. **Intellectualizing**

7. **Diversion**

8. **Passivity**

9. **Hostility**

Exercise # 68

Grief work

Review the three areas of grieving needs below. Identify what areas you need to grieve. Process this with someone who can support you through the grieving process.

Grieving past acting out experiences
Giving up past acting out behaviors is very difficult, especially if they have been occurring for many years. Once you abandon your old ways, you have to grieve them. You have to admit they were once a part of you. You have to stop the comforts that you felt you could only turn to. You have to grieve them so you can move on. Once free, you will feel mourning for the past. You may have had a long term relationship and finally have come to terms that it was not really intended to be. You may mourn for the wasted time you spent on your addiction. You may mourn for all the hurts that you had created for others. You may mourn for the hurt it has caused you.

Grieving lost parenting
As we know, parents have had their roles in the development of addictions. A boy who has been robbed of his father's love and attention will need to mourn this loss. With any loss, mourning must take place. Elizabeth Kubler-Ross has identified stages of the grieving process: denial, anger, bargaining, depression, and acceptance. These are not necessarily fixed and they can be fluid. It helps to be guided through feelings as they surface. For example, a man grieving the loss of parenting by his dad may hold onto anger and need to work through it several times before he can ever get to the stage of acceptance. Acceptance is the final stage and is worth getting to, because it is there where freedom is.

Grieving lost childhood
Many of my clients have a common theme of rejection and a sense of not fitting in while growing up. This has often been accompanied by outward hostile words, physical, mental, emotional, and/or sexual abuse. A child who has been robbed the opportunity to play in the game or to be part of a group has to mourn the loss. A child's true intent is to be adventurous. If this has been taken from him, he has needs to heal from this loss.

Some practice steps to mourning loss:
Set a time to mourn the loss.
Light a candle for your lost object.
Write a letter to the loss.
Bury or burn your letter.
Express your sorrow. Play music that invokes sorrow.
Review how you will accept this loss and how you will move on.

Exercise # 69

Tagging procrastination

One of the barriers to recovery for overcoming addiction is self-defeating procrastination. Many people joke about procrastination, but really it is a serious issue which can yield huge consequences. Psychologist Dr. William Backus, in his book, *Finding the freedom of self control*, lists some common rationalizations for procrastinating.

Review the list given by Dr. Backus and see if any of these apply to you when it comes to doing your recovery work. If so, develop an action plan whereas you challenge the rationalization.

Check list

___I'm too busy.
___I have too many things to do.
___I don't know what to do first.
___I don't have time.
___I can't do it well so I won't do it at all.
___I don't know how.
___I'm not in the mood to do anything I find disagreeable.
___I'm too tired.
___I'm sick of doing that.
___It's too trivial to bother with – other things are more important.
___I should do some other things before I start that.

Processing Questions

1. Which one(s) do you identify with?
2. What plans can you make to defeat procrastination?

Action Plan

____
____
____
____
____
____
____

Exercise # 70

Inventory of how my addiction impacts others

Undoubtedly your addiction has had an impact on someone close to you. A part of recovery is taking an inventory of those we harmed by our addictive behaviors. This exercise will help you to process how your addiction has harmed those close to you. In the exercise below, list your significant others (e.g. spouse, friends, etc.). Give specific examples of the hurtful behavior you have done. A vague example like, "I lied to my wife," is meaningless. For you to really see the impact you must give specific examples like, "I lied to my wife last week. I told her I lost the money but really I went out and bought drugs." You may use the same person more than once.

Significant other	*Harmful behavior*	*Example*
1.		
2.		
3.		
4.		
5.		
6.		
7.		
8.		
9.		
10.		

Exercise # 71

Assertiveness

It is important in recovery to reclaim assertiveness. This is an area that has been lost due to the dynamics of addictions. Assertiveness means standing up for what you think and feel while respecting the autonomy of others. Process the exercise below to have you reclaim your assertiveness.

As a person I have a right to:

1. Be treated with respect.
2. Have and express my own feelings and opinions. For example, using statements such as, "When you____, I feel______."
3. Set my own priorities.
4. Not to be abused.
5. Be listened to and taken seriously.
6. Say no, or hell no, without feeling guilty.
7. Ask for what I want.
8. Make mistakes – and be responsible for them.
9. Feel and express anger.
10. Change my mind.
11. Be myself.
12. Say, "I don't understand."
13. Grow, learn, and change.
14. Say, "I don't have the answer."
15. Say, "I need a break," and take one.
16. Have my needs be as important as the needs of others.
17. Say, "I need some time to think this over."
18. Ask for help.
19. Be given praise and affirmation.
20. Choose not to assert myself when I don't want to.

Exercise # 72

Understanding group dynamics

Group work can be very beneficial in the recovery process. One thing to be conscious of is the various group behaviors that can arise from yourself and other members. Review the following list of commonly seen group behaviors and take the risk to confront them if and when they arise.

1. **Minimizing -** For example: "I only had three beers."
2. **Making fools of others -** By putting others down, we take the focus off ourselves.
3. **Assuming** – For example, "Nobody cares about me anyway." This gives us an excuse to act out, because, "Nobody cares…"
4. **I'm unique** – "No one can tell me what to do." By putting ourselves in a special category, we rob ourselves of help.
5. **Lying** – Confuses, distorts, and takes the focus of the behavior. Subtypes include:

    Commission – making things up that are not true.
    Omission – Leaving out details or sections.
    Assent – presenting others' ideas to look good with no intentions of following through.

6. **Blaming** – Permits the build up of resentments and takes the focus of the addict and puts in on others. For example: "The trouble with you is that you are so critical of me. If you weren't, maybe I wouldn't use drugs so much."
7. **Making excuses** - For example: "I have sex because I am depressed and it makes me feel good," or "The reason I drink is because my husband is so mean to me."
8. **Aggression** – Scaring others by power surges so that they will either agree with us or leave us alone.
9. **Staying in the safety zone** – Withholding information because of the fear of confrontation, embarrassment, or fear of being vulnerable.
10. **Grandiosity** – For example: "I've spilled more booze then you've drank," or "He's had sex with only three people and thinks he's a sex addict."

Exercise # 73

Rules for getting the most out of group

It is undeniably difficult to assimilate in a group setting, especially when it means you must be vulnerable. The following is a good guideline for getting the most out of your group experience:

1. The group as a whole must make a commitment to adhere to confidentiality. That is, what is said in the group stays in the group. It must be a safe container.
2. Participate as fully as possible. The more you put in, the more you'll take out.
3. Feel free to give feedback. Do not pass judgment, but simply state what you see or hear and then what *you* feel.
4. Take "time". Focus on the issues you need to work on.
5. Use "I" statements.
6. Keep an open mind. Be willing to discover positive and negative, growing and limiting sides of yourself.
7. Remember that the group is a place for progress, not perfection. See it as a safe place to grow.
8. Use the group to practice new behaviors. Don't be afraid to ask for help to role-play issues or to use psychodrama to help you express behaviors and emotions.
9. Pay attention to your own body language and feelings. Don't shut them out.
10. Leave your mask and false self outside the group.
11. Avoid postponing the risk taking involved in letting others know you.
12. You "earned" your seat in the group. Don't apologize for your statements.

Exercise # 74

Talking to the group

Talking for the first time in a group is scary. The following outline will help to break the ice and get you talking. It is also an exercise for the others in listening.

Hello, my name is_______________.
The reason I'm here is_____________.
Right now, I'm feeling_____________.

When I'm in a new group, I______________.
When I'm in a new situation, I usually______________.
I'm happiest when_________________.
When I'm alone, I usually_______________.
My biggest worry, right now, is_____________________.

I love____________.
I feel healthy pride when_____________.
I feel sad or blue when___________________.
My feelings get easily hurt when__________________.
I feel embarrassed when__________________.
The last thing in the world I want to do is__________________.

My favorite book is___________________.
My favorite movie is______________________.
The person I miss the most is___________________.

The thing I like best about myself is________________.
Toward you, right now, I feel________________________.
Right now I am feeling____________________.

Exercise # 75

Opening up in a recovery group

Talking in a recovery group or even one on one can be difficult. In this exercise you will be able to identify what is hard to talk about and practice ways to talk more openly. All this will help you on the road of recovery.

1. List 10 things in your life that are difficult to talk about.

2. Put them in order from the least threatening to the most difficult to talk about.

3. Talk with just one person you trust the most about the experience and what you may have learned from the experience.

4. Examine your fears while doing this with the reality of actually doing it. You will find you feel much better after talking!

5. Next, starting with the least threatening issue, talk about it in a group setting. Again, examine your fears while doing this with the reality of actually doing it. You will find you feel much better after talking!

6. Continue each time with addressing another issue on your list. After you have tackled all 10, you will see how much better you feel, less threatened and less fearful.

Exercise # 76

Topics to talk about in group

There are several appropriate things to bring up in the group meeting. For this exercise, review the list of topics that can be talked about in a group. To further this, use them as a guide for your own group process.

1. Difficulty I have in raising my hand to speak
2. Cravings, urges to go back in addiction behaviors
3. Dreams
4. Resistance to coming to group
5. Difficulty asking someone to be sponsor/mentor
6. Problems calling sponsor/mentor
7. Gut feelings
8. Boredom
9. Dealing with using friends or relatives
10. Sober experiences (e.g. things I've done for the time or in a long time sober)
11. Isolating behaviors
12. Making sober friends
13. Breakthrough in denial
14. Problems at home, work, or relationships
15. Consequences
16. The steps
17. Relapse
18. Changes in lifestyles or behaviors
19. Relationship with God
20. Boundaries (See following exercise, next page)

Exercise # 77

Group work on the topic of boundaries

The following is an outline of a group format to use with the topic of boundaries:

Check in: State your name, reason for being here, and how you are doing.

Definition: Our boundaries define how we are able to interact and relate to the world around us.

Physical: Sets our need to physical space and safety. Some physical boundaries are unhealthy, like when someone invades your personal space.

EXERCISE: Look at where you are sitting. Why did you choose that seat? Or:
Think of a time when someone evaded your personal space. What did that look like? How did it make you feel? Can you share what you did?

Sometimes boundaries can be used to protect us from getting to know someone or from allowing someone to get close to us. This boundary sets us up for isolation. This is called "disengagement." Here we develop an overly protective boundary. It is like being surrounded physically and emotionally by a steel capsule.

PROCESS QUESTIONS: Can you relate? Has there been a time when you had to do this?

If you are more of the disengaged type, then: If you want to feel safe, you must be willing to allow ourselves to feel vulnerable at times. Practical: Join a group.

On the other extreme, if you are too "enmeshed" with others, boundaries are burred/distorted and that is unhealthy. In this example, you lack a sense of boundary. Here, "I cannot experience myself as separate from others. It becomes difficult to distinguish myself from others. I feel my feelings and all of your feelings too. I begin to define myself according to your definition. I lose my own identity. My feelings are your feelings, my thoughts are your thoughts and I behave the way I think you want me to"

EXERCISE: Can you relate? Can you think of anyone who is smothering?
During the remainder of the group time, process with each other the thoughts and feelings.

Check out: "I'm checking out with…"

Moment of silence. Give members opportunity to say serenity prayer, speak to their higher power, or remain in relaxed phase until dismissed.

Exercise # 78

Relapse warning signs

There are no automatic guarantees in recovery. You live one day at a time. However, there are some warning signs to relapse, and if you stay conscious of them, you better your opportunity not to relapse. Use the following inventory to identify common relapse warning signs.

_____ Trying to control/ run another's recovery program

_____ Isolation

_____ Depression

_____ Compulsive or impulsive behaviors

_____ Attempts to control people, places, and things

_____ Being defensive

_____ "I don't care" attitude

_____ Taking on the responsibilities of others

_____ Easily angered

_____ Daydreaming

_____ Lying

_____ Holding feelings in

_____ Periods of confusion

_____ Feeling powerless and hopeless

_____ Feeling sorry for myself

_____ Preoccupation with one area of my life

_____ Over-reaction to stressful situations

_____ Over or under sleeping

Exercise #78, Continued

_____ Over or under eating

_____ Loss of daily structure

_____ Feelings of inferiority or superiority

_____ Nagging/whining

_____ Immature wish to be happy or to make others happy

_____ Insensitivity to the feelings of others

_____ Avoiding issues or problems

_____ Try to force sobriety on others

_____ Focusing on the past

_____ Projecting into the future

_____ Not having any fun

_____ Compulsive sexual behavior

_____ Hoarding money or overspending

_____ Increasing physical complaints

_____ Fantasies about the addiction behaviors

_____ Increasing work dissatisfaction

_____ Overconfidence about recovery

_____ Increasing use of non-prescription medication

_____ Rejecting help

_____ Blaming others for my problems

_____ Cutting down or stopping meetings

_____ Resentments

_____ Hanging around addiction stimuli/environments

Exercise #78, Continued

_____ Thinking I am cured

_____ Start using a chemical other than my drug of choice

_____ Convince myself I can practice "controlled" behaviors

_____ Losing control

_____ Deny my fears

_____ See problems as unsolvable

_____ Unrealistic expectations

Exercise # 79

Relapse prevention plan

While relapse may be common for addicts, you do not have to relapse. Preventing relapse requires an awareness of our own denial process and the willingness to do something about it. We need to be vigilant about exposing our denial to ourselves and others.

I. You have the information within yourself that tells you the circumstances which can set you up for relapse. Answer the following questions as honestly as you can.

Who are the people you are most likely to use with?

1.

2.

3.

4.

What feelings place you at greatest risk for using?

1.

2.

3.

What situations or events place you at risk for using? Why?

1.

2.

3.

4.

5.

Exercise #79, Continued

What will be the consequences for you if you relapse?

1.

2.

3.

4.

II. This plan is used in conjunction with your Relapse Warning List. You may use this list as part of a daily inventory to check on your denial status and plan your recovery day around it. Review the list and identify your warning signs. Look at your feelings, thoughts, and behavior, and decide what you will do about it.

Example:

Warning sign:	Hanging around using environments.
Thought/s:	I miss my friends.
Feeling/s:	I feel bored and lonely.
Behavior:	I stopped at the bar just to say hello. I had a soda.
Recovery action:	**a.** Call my sponsor and talk to him/her about it.
	b. Go to a meeting and talk about it.
	c. Make plans to go to a movie with a sober friend in treatment.

Now, outline your own specific plan using:

Warning sign:

Thought/s:

Feeling/s:

Behavior:

Recovery action: **a.**
b.
c.

Exercise #79, Continued

Warning sign:

Thought/s:

Feeling/s:

Behavior:
Recovery action: a.
b.
c.

Warning sign:

Thought/s:

Feeling/s:

Behavior:

Recover action: a.
b.
c.

Warning sign:

Thought/s:

Feeling/s:

Behavior:

Recovery action: a.
b.
c.

Adapted with modifications, from: Olsen, J., Fallon, J., & Mark, L. (1993). *Groups: A manual (and handouts) for chemical dependency and psychiatric treatment.* Sante Fe, NM: CL Productions.

Exercise # 80

Recovery plan outline

The recovery plan is a 90-day contract that you make with yourself, specifically detailing the action that you will take in your recovery. **This is a commitment.** To ensure success it needs to be realistic, so KEEP IT SIMPLE!

A commitment is a decision. The best way to express a commitment is to firmly state what your action will be. The words "I will" shows a decision to follow through with ACTION. For example, note the difference in the following two statements:

1. "I will go to a group meeting every day for 90 days."
2. "I will try to go to a group meeting every day."

In the Step programs they say, *"Trying is lying"* or, *"Trying is dying."* Trying means that there is really no commitment at all! We can always let ourselves off the hook with, *"Oh well, I tried."* Our commitment should be **simple, clean, and realistic**. For instance, if I am considering some form of exercise in my sober program and I have been a "couch potato" for the last five years, then a commitment to run ten miles a day is unreasonable. Instead, I could commit to walking a few blocks every day. This could consist of a ten minute walk each way and my commitment then would be: *"I will walk a total of twenty minutes, five days per week."* Therefore, this statement includes **what I will do** and **how often I will do it**.

The following outline may help to design your own individual recovery plan:

ALWAYS INCLUDE WHAT YOU WILL DO AND HOW OFTEN!!!!

1. Remaining free of addictive behaviors:

Example:

"I will remain chemically free, one day at a time. I will inform my physician that I am a recovering alcoholic. I will inform my dentist that I am a recovering alcoholic. I will check out all medication I may need with my sponsor or the treatment program."

Exercise #80, Continued

2. Meetings: When, where, and how often will you go to meetings?

Example:

"I will attend 90 meetings in 90 days." If you already know that you can't attend a meeting on a certain day, "double up" the following day. Include a tentative meeting schedule.

Example:

"I will attend 90 meetings in 90 days. Every other Monday I have class so I can't make a meeting. Therefore, I will double up meetings on Tuesday by attending the noon and 6 PM meetings."

3. Sponsorship: Who is my sponsor? How often will I contact him/her? If I do not have a sponsor, will I get one? When will I get one?

Examples:

1. If I have a sponsor: My sponsor's name is Ann. I will call her every other day.
2. If I don't have a sponsor: I will have a sponsor in one week.
3. I am moving to Atlanta when I leave treatment. I will have a temporary sponsor within two weeks of my arrival.

4. Working The Steps:

Examples:

1. I will review my Step One with my sponsor next week.
2. I will continue working the Steps and meeting with my sponsor every two weeks.

(Remember, you cannot complete this one unless you have consulted with your sponsor.)

Exercise #80, Continued

5. Spirituality: How do you get in touch with your spiritual self and have time for contemplation? Include a plan for prayer and meditation and/or religious practices, if appropriate.

Examples:

1. I will read _____________ every morning.
2. I will pray every morning and every evening.
3. I will attend church services every two weeks with my family.
4. I will take a walk in the woods once a week.

6. Physical Health: Include commitment for diet, exercise, medical problems.

Examples:

1. I will continue treatment for my gastric ulcer and will follow-up with my physician. I have an appointment on ________________.
2. I will eat at least two healthy meals per day.
3. I will work out at the gym two times per week.
4. I will take my high blood pressure medication as prescribed by my physician.

7. Emotional Health: Include any counseling appointments and the name of the counselor or who you will talk with about your feelings.

Examples:

1. I will talk to my sponsor at least two times per week about my feelings.
2. I will share my feelings with my husband as they come up instead of holding them in.

Exercise #80, Continued

3. I will follow through with my counseling appointment with ___________ on ___________.

Identify the feeling that is most difficult for you to deal with.

Examples: Anger

When you are angry, what will you do to deal with it?

1. Go to group and talk about it.

2. Call my sponsor, mentor, or a sober friend.

3. When I have a fight with my wife, I will go for a ten minute walk to calm down.

4. I will practice the anger exercises in my workbook.

8. Employment: What are your work plans? Since overworking is often a compulsive behavior and can interfere with your program, what is the maximum number of hours you will work per week?

Examples:

1. If overworking is a problem: I will return to my job and will not work over 45 hours in a week.

2. If unemployment is a problem: I will begin looking for a job in one week. I will apply to at least two places per week.

3. If my job is unhealthy: I will quit my bartending job immediately.

9. Legal Issues: Include court dates and planning.

Examples:

1. I will attend my DUI hearing on _____________.

2. I have an appointment with my lawyer on ____________.

Exercise #80, Continued

3. I have no legal issues pending.

10. Family Relationships: Include a plan for activities with family members **and** a plan for dealing with using family members.

Examples:

1. I will go out to dinner or to a movie with my wife once a week.

2. I will plan an activity with my children every Saturday.

3. I will call my brother and tell him I cannot have drinking in my house when he comes to visit.

4. I will not attend my cousin's wedding next week since there will be alcohol there.

11. Social Growth: This is a plan for developing sober relationships and for detaching from using ones. What will you do to make sober friends?

Examples:

1. I will call Jake from my treatment group two times a week.

2. I will go out for coffee with my sponsor or safe friend one time a week.

3. I will go to a recovery conference in Phoenix in October.

4. I will contact Lenny to tell him that I quit my addiction and that I won't be around anymore.

12. Leisure Time: What will you do for fun? What interests or hobbies do you plan on resuming now that you are sober?

Examples:

1. I will go fishing at least once a month.

Exercise #80, Continued

2. I will attend art classes one time per week.

3. I will hike every two weeks with a friend.

4. I will practice my guitar twice a week for one hour.

13. Fire Drill: This is your action plan for when you feel like acting out again.

Example:

1. I will call my sponsor, accountability partner.

2. I will double up my meetings for three days and talk about my craving.

3. I will read recovery based literature.

4. I will talk about it with my wife/husband.

5. I will read my Step One.

14. Relapse Plan: If I use, what can I do **now** to keep me in recovery?

Examples:

1. Call my sponsor or alternate if my sponsor is not available.

2. Tell my family within 24 hours.

3. Restart 90 meetings in 90 days, or restart a recovery group most associated with my particular addiction.

4. Tell my Aftercare Group.

The shame of relapse can keep you using. It will only get smaller if you let someone know what happened.

Adapted with modifications, from: Olsen, J., Fallon, J., & Mark, L. (1993). *Groups: A manual (and handouts) for chemical dependency and psychiatric treatment.* Sante Fe, NM: CL Productions.

Exercise # 81

Recovery plan worksheet

Now that you have reviewed the way a plan should look, personalize a realistic one for yourself. Make sure to designate someone to keep you accountable. Give that person a copy of your plan as well.

1. Remaining chemically free:

2. Meeting/Group:

DAY	TIME	LOCATION
Sunday		
Monday		
Tuesday		
Wednesday		
Thursday		
Friday		
Saturday		

3. Sponsorship:

4. Working the Steps:

Exercise #81, Continued

5. Spiritual Practice:

6. Physical Health:

7. Emotional Health:

The emotion that places me at greatest risk for reactive behavior is:

When I feel _____________, I will:

a.

b.

c.

8. Employment:

9. Legal Issues:

10. Family Relationships:

11. Social Growth:

Exercise #81, Continued

12. Leisure Activities:

13. Fire Drill: Five things I will do if I want to use:

a.

b.

c.

d.

e.

14. Relapse Plan: Things that I will do if I relapse:

a.

b.

c.

d.

e.

Adapted with modifications, from: Olsen, J., Fallon, J., & Mark, L. (1993). *Groups: A manual (and handouts) for chemical dependency and psychiatric treatment.* Sante Fe, NM: CL Productions.

Exercise # 82

Looking at addictive behaviors: Inside and outside perspectives

We must keep a fearless inventory of those addictive behaviors that we often seek. Just as important is getting an outsider/objective point of view. In this exercise, you will confront those addiction-seeking behaviors that are familiar to you and at the same time get the views of those close to you.

1. List your behaviors that your feel are addiction seeking.

2. Meet with four community members who know you and your addiction and ask them to describe what they see as addiction seeking behaviors.

3. Compare your list with your peers' observations and discuss as a group.

4. Share your list and ask others for feedback.

5. Share what you learned.

Exercise # 83

Honesty about my addiction: What does it *really* look like?

Here is an exercise for you to complete which will give you a chance to be completely honest about what you look like (thoughts, behaviors, ideas, feelings, etc.) when under the influence of your addiction. For an alcoholic, he may list the type of person he is when he is drunk, what things he has done while drunk, and what others say about him when he is drunk.

1. Describe what kind of person you are (behaviorally) when you are under the influence of your addiction.
2. What are the feelings you encounter under that situation?
3. What are your thoughts about when this is happening?
4. What is the worst thing that has happened to you under this influence?
5. Share this with someone or a group for accountability and feedback.

Exercise # 84

What causes me emotional pain?

It is important to be able to identify your emotional pain and its sources. It is also good to be able to establish a supportive network in which to share this pain. Finally, expressing the pain is one way of healing it. This exercise will help you to accomplish this.

1. Identify and rank five things or events in your life that have and continue to cause you the most emotional pain.

2. Explain to someone or group how you dealt with the pain.

3. Next, ask them for feedback. If they have shared the same or similar pain, ask them how they dealt with it.

4. How can you put this information to use to help you?

5. If you could express your pain, how would you do it?

Exercise # 85

Keep a mood log

Keeping a mood log will help you to track your feelings. In this exercise you will be able to list your moods throughout the day, along with what time of day they occurred, what your were doing at the time, who was around, whether or not your talked about it, your affect, and what you did (intervention). If you did nothing, then you can plan an intervention for the future. The log also helps you to see any patterns that may be occurring.

Mood	**Time**	**Behavior**	**People**	**Discuss**	**Affect**	**Intervention**	**Plan**
Ex: Sad	8 pm	I was watching TV	Husband	I didn't talk about it	Some tears; sad look	I did nothing	Talk to a friend, journal

Exercise # 86

Building trust

Many addicts do not trust. This often stems from childhood experiences. As adults in addictions, it can be used as a way of protection and as a way to continue in the addiction. Part of the healing process is trusting others to help you and to let go of the past. In this exercise you can process what trust means to you and how you can obtain it in your life.

1. What is the connection, or lack of connection, of trusting others and addiction?

2. What does trust mean to you?

3. Write an inventory of all the experiences you had trusting others.

4. Ask those of whom you are going through recovery with, "Why should I trust you?"

5. What are your reservations about trust? What holds you back from being fully trustful of others?

6. What are some ways to increase your trust? Can you start asking for what you need?

Exercise # 87

Getting real

The work of getting real is about paying attention to and communicating about what you notice in yourself. This encompasses your bodily sensations, your feelings, your thoughts, and the things going on around you – your awareness. The work or practical application of getting real is sharing with others how you experience your awareness. When we interact with others, we are bound to get bodily sensations, feelings, or thoughts. Allowing ourselves to be aware of these is the first step to getting real. After such, comes the work. That is, sharing with others what is going on within us. The problem, according to Campbell (2001), is that we often stuff our real data. She says, "Instead of sharing our feelings and thoughts, we try to ensure a predictable outcome" (p. 3). The latter, of course, is unhealthy. In those cases we disconnect from the truth of the situation and the truth of our own feelings. Campbell goes on to say that if we persist on trying to get our relationships to conform to our expectations, instead of letting them be how they actually are, we miss the important opportunities to know ourselves and others more deeply. Getting real is about relating. Examine the outlining 10 skills and practice them:

1. *Experiencing what is. What is* refers to whatever is actually going on in the present moment – in our body, mind, and environment. Campbell stressed that we must practice distinguishing between what we actually experience in our body from what our mind thinks, judges, expects, or predicts.
2. *Being transparent.* This involves the use of self-disclosure, which is the ability to reveal to another person what we have done or what we are sensing, feeling, thinking, or saying to ourselves at the moment.
3. *Noticing your intent.* Be spontaneous and unrehearsed in relating to others to get the real emotional affect. Don't communicate with the intent to control the outcome. Let the outcome evolve out of the relationship.
4. *Welcome feedback.* Be actively curious about how others are affected by you. Ask questions such as, "How are you with what I did?"
5. *Assert what you want and do not want.* Asserting what we want affirms our right to want what we want even if that means we may not get it. We must also be able to refuse to do, receive, or speak about something that is not our genuine response.
6. *Taking back projections.* Often what we see in another person is actually a mirror of something in ourselves that we are uncomfortable with. When a timid person is put off by someone aggressive, perhaps he disowns his own aggressiveness. Becoming aware of projections helps us to season our judgments with humility. It should serve to remind us that other's judgments of us are as much about them as they are about us.
7. *Revising an earlier statement.* We have to be flexible to go back and let someone know when our feelings have changed, e.g. as to clear things up.
8. *Holding differences.* This involves allowing us to embrace our own viewpoints while at the same time being open to hearing and considering differing views.
9. *Sharing mixed emotions.* It's okay to be both angry and afraid. We should share both. This skill teaches you to let go of your ideas and shoulds about being consistent so that you can experience whatever shows up in your awareness.
10. *Embracing the silence.* Get in the moment – silence is connection. Don't try to predict an outcome, just allow yourself to feel.

Reference: Campbell, S. (2001). Getting Real. Tiburon, CA: HJ Kramer

Exercise # 88

Journaling

During recovery you will need to release thoughts and feelings in a constructive, safe way. Journaling is one way to help bring unconscious material conscious. It helps us to be present. It is a tool to gain insight into oneself.

1. Use the journaling sheets provided at the end of this workbook to journal your thoughts and feelings. You may also find it helpful to purchase a separate notebook to do this exercise.

2. Allow whatever you are feeling to surface without thinking about it-just let it come.

3. Put your feelings into words and write them down without trying to sound proper or nice; editing and grammar is not necessary. Do not distract the real emotions from coming.

Exercise # 89

Relieving boredom

Many people feel a void once they are in the recovery process. They have changed many of their addictive behaviors and now they have become bored. Can you relate to this? In this exercise, you will challenge yourself to do something productive to rid yourself of post addiction boredom. A few examples are provided. What will you do? An application section is also provided to help you.

Learn something new: Your brain is longing to learn something new. Lifelong learning is one of the cornerstones to mental acuity. Take a class. Try a new sport. Read a different book. It's an easy way to break through your boredom. Talk to someone new: new people bring new ideas. Ask the person next to you on the elevator what they did this weekend. Talk with your receptionist when you enter the office. Make the effort to speak with someone new this week.

Solve a problem: Try a crossword puzzle or suduku. Look for a logic puzzle on-line or read a difficult mystery. Spending time today trying to solve a puzzle will help to relieve your boredom and activate active problem solving.

Take in some of the arts: Watch a play or ballet. Visit your local art museum or natural history museum. Take in an IMAX film. New stimulation will bring new thoughts and stop the repeating thoughts. When you find yourself repeating thoughts, remind yourself to get present by focusing on what is right in front of you. With a little work, you will begin to feel your mind awaken. Awakening your mind helps guarantee long-term mental health. It's worth the effort (Ref: Editor, (2006, Jan). Boredom. *Open Grove Newletter, 5*(7c), 1).

Application:

1. These are the voids in my life:____
____
____
2. What are some things I can do to help fill the voids in my life?________________
____
____

2. Whom can I invite into my life to help me? ______________________________
____
3. What are some obstacles I need to overcome? ____________________________
____
4. My plan to make this possible:____

Exercise # 90

Mirroring

In this exercise you will take a good look at yourself in the mirror. This exercise is aimed toward helping you gain information about yourself by looking and seeing what really lies beneath your face.

1. Find a mirror to look into. You should be comfortable whether you are standing or sitting.
2. Be centered and allow yourself to look at yourself in the mirror.
3. Observe your eyes and all the features of your face. Notice any facial projects.
4. Allow the feelings that are evoked by looking at yourself to surface.
5. Log the feelings.
6. Talk to yourself and tell yourself what you need to hear.

Exercise # 91

Identifying old rules: Rule no more!

In this exercise you will identify and clarify those old rules that you carry in your psyche that have been handed down to you from others, usually your parents. You will weed out dysfunctional messages and let them go. It will help you to distinguish between your own feelings and those handed down to you from others.

1. List those who raised you and who had strong influence of authority in your life.

2. Beneath each person, write whatever adjectives come to mind that apply to that person (e.g. bossy, sad, angry, manipulative, etc.).

3. Under each person, list several unspoken rules. This means anything that you knew to do, think, or feel, or not to do, think, or feel.

4. Go back to the lists and circle any that apply to you. Circle any that you feel you still live by or pass on.

5. Discuss how you feel these rules apply to you and how you feel they have affected you.

Exercise # 92

Surrendering to reality

In the Narcotics Anonymous (1982), they have a saying that, "recovery begins with surrender" (p. 86). Without our addictions, we have a chance to function as useful human beings if we accept ourselves and the world as it is. Part of the surrender is facing reality, facing the problems and limitation in our lives. In this exercise, you will be guided through some questions to help you process surrender and reality.

1. What is it about reality you dislike?
2. What are the conflicts you face about reality?
3. What areas in your life do you need to surrender?
4. Can you be satisfied with not having all the answers or solutions?

Exercise # 93

"Hugs not drugs" (or other addictions)

According to Narcotics Anonymous (NA) (1982), "Recovery becomes a contact process; we lose the fear of touching and being touched. We learn that a simple, loving hug can make all the difference in the world when we feel alone. We experience real love and real friendship" (p. 88). In this exercise, you will discover your comfort level around the issue of nonsexual affection and touch.

1. How do you react to the quote by NA?

2. What fears do touch and affection bring for you?

3. What prohibitions around affection do you have?

4. What was affection like for you growing up?

5. Have you ever had touch boundaries violated?

6. Read Keating, K. (1983). The hug therapy book. Minneapolis: CompCare.

7. Processing affirmation:

   Today I will nurture my inner child and myself by giving and receiving physical affection. Resisting affection had been my way to stay disconnected and uninvolved with others. Today I give myself freedom to express affection and not feel shame. It does not have to be sexual, rather it is human. Thoughts that this is wrong may be other's truths, but not mine. I own my needs for safe, nonsexual, human touch. I will be still in my mind of negative projections about others and allow myself to feel safe, loved, and cared for. Today I will reach out and celebrate my ability to touch and to be touched.

Exercise # 94

Sleep

Recovery is hard work. Addictions have taken their toll. Sleep is a well-needed friend. This exercise is designed to help you affirm the need to mentally let go so you allow your self the ability to sleep, without guilt. Process this daily affirmation below:

> Recovery is hard work. It's hard on the body, the mind, and the emotions. Sometimes I feel like I need to sleep for a week just to catch up, but so much needs to be done. So I drink coffee, or I________________ (fill in the blank) to keep awake and keep going. I'm exhausted!
>
> ***As a loving and responsible parent, I know my inner child needs plenty of rest to grow and develop. So I make sure that he gets to bed on time and that bed is a place of comfort and renewal. I tell him it's okay to get as much sleep as he needs. I help him crawl into bed and wrap himself up warmly in the covers. I hold him a he drifts off to sleep. He sleeps until his body signals it's time to wake and he wakes refreshed and ready to start a new day.***

(Adapted from "I let myself get as much sleep as I need," Lerner, R. (1990). *Affirmation for the inner child.* Deerfield, FL: Health Communications, Inc.)

Exercise # 95

Social life affirmation

In our addictions we have burned many bridges. It has left us empty of real, healthy relationships. Part of recovery is rebuilding those bridges. One way is to affirm our need to be a social person. Practice the affirmation below and go forth to make it a reality in your life. The results will be amazing.

I will celebrate my attractiveness as a person by creating a satisfying social life for myself. Outings, parties and entertainment in the company of others can enrich my life.

A healthy social life was virtually nonexistent when I was addicted. Inwardly I was consumed by my addiction and I isolated myself from the real world. I rarely risked inviting friends to visit me. As a result, I grew into not having any real experiences of a normal, satisfying social life. I often spent my leisure time alone because social events were simply too uncomfortable for me.

As I grow toward wholeness, I feel the desire to be with healthy others. I find that enjoying the company of friends fills deep needs in my soul. Today I will go about the business of creating a satisfying social life.

(Adapted from "I can create a satisfying social life," Lerner, R. (1990). *Affirmation for the inner child.* Deerfield, FL: Health Communications, Inc.)

Exercise # 96

Dealing with your fear of failure

You might be afraid of offending someone or hurting someone's feelings. Many people want to have the nicest things and struggle to make everything perfect. The fear of failure lingers over much of what we think and do. Under the influence of this fear, we often eat, drink, and spend too much. We injure our bodies, spirits, minds, and pocket books in an effort to create a perfect life. The fear of failure stems from being disconnected from the reality of your life and focusing on the fantasy of what you believe your life should look like. This disconnect may stem from critical or violent voices in your childhood or possibly your own desire to be cooler, wealthier, or something that you were not as a child. Regardless of where this fear came from, it's time to let it go.

This is a writing exercise. Feel free to use your journal, computer, or notebook. Let's understand your fear of failure. Spend time answering the question, "Where does this fear come from?" Go into detail. It's okay to write about it over the course of a couple of days. Be sure to include whether your parents or friends also hold this fear.

1. *Figure out how this fear works in your present life.* Next, answer the question, "How does the fear of failure serve you?" If you get stuck, ask the people who know you well. They might notice things that you are unaware of. Spend time really thinking about all the ways that this fear manifests itself in your current life.

2. What happens if your fear disappears? Imagine a miracle happened and your fear of failure disappeared. What would you lose? Spend time writing and answering the question, "What would I give up if I wasn't afraid of failing anymore?"

3. *What will it take to forgive yourself?* Most people who are afraid of failure struggle to forgive themselves for previous failures. They hold themselves up to an unattainable standard and refuse to accept their own limitations. This painful process creates tremendous rigidity in life. Ask yourself the question, "What will it take to forgive myself?"

Reference: Editor, (2005, Dec). Fear. *The Open Grove Mini Newsletter, 5*(1.6a), 1.

Exercise # 97

Centering

In this exercise you will connect with your body and mind. You will become present and relaxed in the situation.

1. Sit in a chair with your back straight or lie flat on the floor with your palms facing the ceiling. You can do this in silence or with affirmation tapes or music.

2. Focus your attention on the center of your chest, or some other safe focal point.

3. Breath in and out easily and completely. The inhalation should be shorter than the exhalation.

4. On the exhalation, think of pushing the air out completely and in the inhalation, allow the breath to re-enter the body.

5. Imagine the inhalation as being ease and light and the exhalation as a release of toxic energy.

Do this until you feel centered and relaxed.

Exercise # 98

Nurturing yourself

Nurturing yourself has tremendous benefits in the recovery process. It helps to alleviate the stress that you face daily. Here are five steps toward nurturing yourself that you can practice:

1. *Discover what feels nurturing to you* – try journaling to remember times in which you felt particularly nurtured. Gently ask yourself, "what feels nurturing?" After you discover what is nurturing for you, take the time to invest in it.

2. *Resolve any conflicts around nurturing yourself* – discuss your goal of nurturing yourself with the people around you so that they support you in your efforts to nurture yourself.

3. *Give yourself permission to do what feels nurturing* – create the time, space, and energy to nurture yourself by simply giving yourself the permission to do it.

4. *Evaluate if something was nurturing or not* – spend some time evaluating whether your efforts are working.

5. *Be patient with yourself and other people* – like anything new, learning to nurture yourself takes time and effort. Be patient with yourself, and your family, as you learn to nurture yourself (Reference: Editor, (March 16, 2004). *The Open Grove Newsletter,3* (I-12), 2).

6. *Practice affirmation*:

    For as long as I can remember, I have lived my life for others. Pleasing others was of utmost importance in my struggle to protect my emotional and physical well-being.

    As an adult child, I lived my life for others in an attempt to gain approval and love. I consistently put others' needs ahead of my own.

    Now I know that living my life solely to please others is emotional starvation. Like any addiction, my enslavement demanded I give up more and more of me and take less in return.

    Today I will begin to recover from my addiction. I will consider my own needs, desires, and preferences first. Today I will take care of me.

Adapted from Lerner, R. (1990). *Affirmations for the inner child.* Deerfield, FL: Health Communication.

Exercise # 99

Asking for forgiveness

Asking for forgiveness is part of a healthy recovery. In step eight of the Twelve Step Traditions, it states that someone in recovery should be willing to make amends when possible. Here are the four steps in asking for forgiveness.

1. *Acknowledge the injury.* It's important to start by acknowledging that you have injured someone. A simple, "I know that I hurt your feelings," can make a world of difference.

2. *Ask the injured what it was like for them.* It's important to understand in what way your mistake injured the other person. People are very different. The same mistake can injure people in a wide variety of ways. Taking the time to understand the manner in which you injured someone else increases empathy in your relationship. Ask what hurt. Nothing is more frustrating than being told how you were hurt by someone who gets it wrong! Repeat back what you heard to make sure you did not miss anything. Open your heart to hear the actual injury.

3. *Apologize for the injury*. Be specific. Make sure to include all the ways that you injured the other person. A real apology might sound like, "I am sorry that I hurt your feelings and you felt stupid when I ignored you at dinner." A real apology includes, "I am sorry" for a "specific injury" at a "specific time".

4. *Ask the injured how you can make it better*. When we feel guilty, we often desperately want to repair the relationship. In our anxiety and fear of losing the relationship, we make up ways to repair the relationship. Stop working so hard. Ask the injured what you can do to regain their trust. Most people have a clear idea of what you can do; ask them. Follow these easy steps and watch your relationships improve. Apologies are the backbone of relationships. This simple skill will greatly impact all of your relationships. Start today. You are bound to make some mistake today. Practice your new skill. You'll be surprised at the results.

Reference: Editor, The lost art of apology. *The Open Grove*, 5(9B), 1.

Exercise # 100

Good-bye letter to your addiction

Whether you like to think of it this way of not, you have had a relationship with your addiction. It has been an arena full of excitements and let downs. It has occupied a lot of your time, whether it was in your head or in acting-out activities. At some point you have to put an end to your relationship with it. It is much like a divorce. While it is best to leave it, there will be some pain involved. It is a voluntary decision. If you are ready to say goodbye to it, then write a good-bye letter. Tell it what it did to you, what you won't miss, and the new joy you'll have. Share your grief, what you'll miss about it, what adaptations it served for you. Tell it how it has been replaced. Finally, tell it how it needs to go way and how you will live your life without it.

Dear addiction:_______________

FINAL Exercise, Exercise # 101

Become a champion for change

After you have faced growth and change, you will want to give back. In this exercise you will think about ways to give back to others that which you have gained for yourself.

Some ideas include:

Shout for joy!
Start a support group.
Become a mentor.
Give to groups that assist and advocate change.
Share your story with an individual or any size audience.
Volunteer at a recovery seminar or retreat. Give back!
Write and share your story.
Partner with others to build a stronger community.
Encourage others.
Build bridges, highways, and reach for the sky!

"One person's dream will be another person's reality."
-Anonymous

Bibliography

Alcoholics Anonymous. (1975). *Living Sober*. New York: Author.

Alcoholics Anonymous (2007). The Big Book (online version): http://www.alcoholics-anonymous.org/bigbookonline/

Arterburn, S. & Felton, J. (1991). *Toxic Faith*. Nashville: Oliver-Nelson.

Bradshaw, J. (1987). *Healing the shame that binds you*. Deerfield Beach, FL: Health Communications.

Bradshaw, J. (1992). *Homecoming: Reclaiming and championing your inner child.* New York: Bantam Doubleday Dell.

Benson, A. L. (2000). *I shop therefore I am: Compulsive buying and the search for self.* Northvale, NJ: Jason Aronson.

Burns, D (1989). *The feeling good handbook.* New York: Quill/HarperCollins

Burns, D. (1993). Ten days to self esteem. New York: Quill/HarperCollins.

Backus, W. (1987). *Finding the freedom of self control*. Minneapolis: Bethany House.

Capacchione, L. (1991). *Recovery of your inner child.* New York: Fireside Books.

Campbell, S. (2001). *Getting real.* Tiburon, CA: HJ Kramer

Carnes, P. (1992). *Out of the shadows: Understanding sexual addiction.* Center City, MN: Hazelden.

Fanning, P. & O'Neill, J. T. (2004). *The addiction workbook: A step-by-step guide to quitting alcohol and drugs*. Oakland, CA: New Harbinger.

Fossum, M. A. & Mason, M. J. (1986). *Facing shame: Families in recovery*. New York: W. W. Norton.

Gorski, T. T. (1989). *Passages through time: An action plan for preventing relapse.* New York: Harper/Hazelden.

Greenberger, D. & Padesky, C. A. (1995). *Mind over mood.* New York: Guilford Press.

Horvath, T. (2004). *Sex, drugs, gambling, and chocolate.* Atascadero, CA: Impact Publishers.

Katherine, A. (1991). *Anatomy of a food addiction: An effective program to overcome compulsive eating.* Carlsbad, CA: Gurze Books.

Lerner, R. (1990). *Affirmation for the inner child.* Deerfield, FL: Health Communications, Inc.

Marlatt, G.A., & Daley, D. C. (1997). *Managing your drug or alcohol problem: Client workbook.* San Antonio: Psychological Corporation.

Miller, A. (1996). *The drama of the gifted child: The search for the true self.* New York: Basic Books.

Minirth, F. B. (1981). *The workaholic and his family.* Grand Rapids, MI: Baker.

Narcotics Anonymous (1982). *The blue book.* Chatsworth CA: Narcotics Anonymous.

Noll, S. (1992) *Songs for the inner child* [CD]. Santa Fe, NM: Singing Heart Productions.

Perkinson, R. R. (2003). *The gambling addiction patient workbook.* Thousand Oaks, CA: Sage.

Potter-Efron, R. & Potter-Efron, P. (1989). *Letting go of shame: Understanding how shame affects your life.* Center City, MN: Hazelden.

Rogers, R. L. & McMillin, C. S. (1992). *Relapse traps: How to avoid the 12 most common pitfalls in recovery.* New York: Bantam.

Schaeffer, B. (1997). *Is it love, or is it addiction?* Center City, MN: Hazelden.

Schaeffer, B. (1998). *Inner reflections: Meditations for the body and heart* [CD]. Center City, MN: Hazelden.

Twerski, A. (1990). *Addictive thinking: Understanding self deception.* New York: Harper/Hazelden.

Weiser, J. (1993). *Phototherapy techniques: Exploring the secrets of personal snapshots and family albums*. San Francisco: Jossey-Bass.

Note: Materials listed in bibliography are suggestions and references only and do not necessarily indicate author or publisher's endorsements.

Appendix A

Feelings listing

Abandoned
Abused
Aching
Accepted
Accused
Accepting
Admired
Adored
Adventurous
Affectionate
Agony
Alienated
Aloof
Aggravated
Agreeable
Aggressive
Alive
Alone
Alluring
Amazed
Amused
Angry
Anguished
Annoyed
Anxious
Apart
Apathetic
Apologetic
Appreciated
Appreciative
Apprehensive
Appropriate
Approved
Argumentative
Aroused
Astonished
Assertive
Attached
Attacked
Attentive
Attractive
Aware
Awestruck
Badgered
Baited
Bashful
Battered
Beaten
Beautiful
Belligerent
Belittled
Bereaved
Betrayed
Bewildered
Blamed
Blaming
Bonded
Bored
Bothered
Brave
Breathless
Bristling
Broken-up
Bruised
Bubbly
Burdened
Burned
Callous
Calm
Capable
Captivated
Carefree
Careful
Careless
Caring
Cautious
Certain
Chased
Cheated
Cheerful
Childlike
Choked-up
Close
Cold
Comfortable
Comforted
Competent
Competitive
Complacent
Complete
Confident
Confused
Considerate
Consumed
Content
Cool
Courageous
Courteous
Coy
Crabby
Cranky
Crazy
Creative
Critical
Criticized
Cross
Crushed
Cuddly
Curious
Cut
Damned
Dangerous
Daring
Dead
Deceived
Deceptive
Defensive
Delicate
Delighted
Demeaned
Demoralized
Dependent
Depressed
Deprived
Deserted
Desirable
Desired
Despair
Despondent
Destroyed
Different
Dirty
Disenchanted
Disgusted
Disinterested
Dispirited
Distressed
Distrustful
Distrusted
Disturbed
Dominated
Domineering
Doomed
Doubtful
Dreadful
Eager
Ecstatic
Edgy
Edified
Elated
Embarrassed
Empowered
Empty
Enraged
Enraptured
Enthusiastic
Enticed
Esteemed
Exasperated
Excited
Exhilarated
Exposed
Fake
Fascinated
Ferocious
Foolish
Forced
Forceful
Forgiven
Free
Friendly
Frightened
Frustrated
Full
Funny
Furious
Generous
Gentle
Genuine
Giddy

Giving	Irresponsible	Pleased	Self-conscious
Goofy	Irritable	Positive	Selfish
Grateful	Irritated	Powerless	Separated
Greedy	Isolated	Present	Sensuous
Grief	Jealous	Precious	Sexy
Grim	Jittery	Pressured	Shattered
Grimy	Joyous	Pretty	Shocked
Grouchy	Lively	Proud	Shot down
Grumpy	Lonely	Pulled apart	Shy
Hard	Loose	Put down	Sickened
Harried	Lost	Puzzled	Silly
Hassled	Loving	Quarrelsome	Sincere
Healthy	Low	Quiet	Sinking
Helpful	Lucky	Raped	Smart
Helpless	Lustful	Ravished	Smothered
Hesitant	Mad	Ravishing	Smug
High	Maudlin	Real	Sneaky
Hollow	Malicious	Refreshed	Snowed
Honest	Mean	Regretful	Soft
Hopeful	Miserable	Rejected	Solid
Hopeless	Misunderstood	Rejuvenated	Solitary
Horrified	Moody	Rejecting	Sorry
Hostile	Morose	Relaxed	Spacey
Humiliated	Mournful	Relieved	Special
Hurried	Mystified	Remarkable	Spiteful
Hurt	Nasty	Remembered	Spontaneous
Hyper	Nervous	Removed	Squelched
Ignorant	Nice	Repulsed	Starved
Ignored	Numb	Repulsive	Stiff
Immature	Nurtured	Resentful	Stifled
Impatient	Nuts	Resistant	Stimulated
Important	Obsessed	Responsible	Strangled
Impotent	Offended	Responsive	Strong
Impressed	Open	Repressed	Stubborn
Incompetent	Ornery	Respected	Stuck
Incomplete	Out of control	Restless	Stunned
Independent	Overcome	Revolved	Stupid
Insecure	Overjoyed	Rotten	Subdued
Innocent	Overpowered	Ruined	Submissive
Insignificant	Overwhelmed	Sad	Successful
Insincere	Pampered	Safe	Suffocated
Isolated	Panicked	Satiated	Sure
Inspired	Paralyzed	Satisfied	Sweet
Insulted	Paranoid	Scared	Sympathy
Interested	Patient	Scolded	Tainted
Intimate	Peaceful	Scorned	Tearful
Intolerant	Pensive	Scrutinized	Tender
Involved	Perceptive	Secure	Tense
Irate	Perturbed	Seduced	Terrific
Irrational	Phony	Seductive	Terrified
Irked	Pleasant	Self-centered	Thrilled

Ticked
Tickled
Tight
Timid
Tired
Tolerant
Tormented
Torn
Tortured
Touched
Trapped
Tremendous
Tricked
Trusted
Trusting
Ugly

Unacceptable
Unapproachable
Unaware
Uncertain
Uncomfortable
Under control
Understanding
Understood
Undesirable
Unfriendly
Ungrateful
Unified
Unhappy
Unimpressed
Unsafe
Unstable

Upset
Uptight
Used
Useful
Useless
Unworthy
Validated
Valuable
Valued
Victorious
Violated
Violent
Voluptuous
Vulnerable
Warm
Wary

Weak
Whipped
Whole
Wicked
Wild
Willing
Wiped out
Wishful
Withdrawn
Wonderful
Worried
Worthy
Zany

Appendix B

Activities list

Meeting someone new
Going to a concert
Playing baseball or softball
Planning trips or vacations
Buying things for myself
Being at the beach
Doing artwork (painting, sculpture, drawing, movie-making, etc.)
Rock climbing or mountaineering
Reading the Scriptures or other sacred works
Playing golf
Taking part in military activities
Rearranging or redecorating my room or house
Going to a sports event
Reading a "How to Do It" book or article
Going to the races (horse, car, boat, etc.)
Reading stories, novels, non-fiction poems, or plays
Going to lectures or hearing speakers
Thinking up or arranging a song or music
Boating (canoeing, kayaking, motor-boating, sailing, etc.)
Restoring antiques, refinishing furniture, etc.
Watching TV
Camping
Working in politics
Working on machines (cars, bikes, motorcycles, tractors, etc.)
Thinking about something good in the future
Playing cards
Completing a difficult task
Laughing
Solving a problem, puzzle, crossword, etc.
Being at weddings, baptisms, confirmations, etc.
Having lunch with friends or associates
Playing tennis
Driving long distances
Woodworking, carpentry
Writing stories, novels, plays, or poetry
Being with animals
Riding in an airplane
Exploring (hiking away from known routes, spelunking, etc.)
Having a frank and open conversation
Singing in a group
Going to church functions (socials, classes, bazaars, etc.)

Speaking a foreign language
Going to service, civic, or social club meetings
Going to a business meeting or a convention
Playing a musical instrument
Making snacks
Snow skiing
Being helped
Being with friends
Solving a personal problem
Being in a city
Taking a bath
Singing to myself
Making food or crafts to sell or give away
Playing pool or billiards
Playing with children
Playing chess or checkers
Doing craft work (pottery, jewelry, leather, beads, weaving, etc.)
Designing or drafting
Visiting people who are sick, shut in, or in trouble
Cheering, rooting
Bowling
Being popular at a gathering
Watching wild animals
Having an original idea
Gardening, landscaping, or doing yard work
Reading essays or technical academic, or professional literature
Wearing new clothes
Riding in a motorcycle
Just sitting and thinking
Seeing good things happen to my family or friends
Going to a fair, carnival, circus, zoo, or amusement park
Talking about philosophy or religion
Planning or organizing something
Listening to the sounds of nature
Dating, courting, etc.
Having a lively talk
Having friends come to visit
Playing in a sporting competition
Introducing people I think would like each other
Giving gifts
Going to school or government meetings, court sessions, etc
Getting massages or backrubs with safe people/professionals
Getting letters, cards, or notes
Watching the sky, clouds, or a storm
Going on outings (to the park, a picnic, a barbecue, etc.)
Playing basketball

Buying something for my family
Photography
Giving a speech or lecture
Reading maps
Gathering natural objects (wild foods or fruit, rocks, driftwood, etc.)
Working on my finances
Helping someone
Being in the mountains
Getting a job advancement (being promoted, given a raise, or offered a better job; getting accepted to a better school, etc.)
Hearing jokes
Meeting someone new
Going to a revival or crusade
Seeing beautiful scenery
Eating good meals
Improving my health (having my teeth fixes, getting new glasses, changing my diet, etc.)
Wrestling or boxing
Hunting or shooting
Playing in a musical group
Hiking
Going to a museum or exhibit
Writing papers, essays, articles, reports, memos, etc.
Doing a job well
Having spare time
Fishing
Loaning something
Going to a health club, sauna bath, etc.
Learning to do something new
Going to a "drive-thru" (Dairy Queen, McDonalds, etc.)
Horseback riding
Protesting social, political, or environmental conditions
Talking on the telephone to a supportive person
Kicking leaves, sand, pebbles, etc.
Playing lawn sports (badminton, croquet, shuffleboard, horseshoes, etc.)
Going to school reunions, alumni meetings, etc.
Seeing famous people
Going to the movies
Budgeting my time
Cooking meals
Being praised by people I admire
Feeling the presence of God in my life
Doing a project my own way
Doing "odd jobs" around the house
Crying
Being told that I am needed
Being at a family reunion or get-together

Giving a party or get-together
Coaching someone
Seeing or smelling a flower or plant
Being invited out
Having someone agree with me
Reminiscing, talking about old times
Getting up early in the morning
Having peace and quiet
Doing experiments or other scientific work
Visiting friends
Writing in a diary
Playing football
Saying prayers
Meditating or doing yoga
Doing favors for people
Talking with people on the job or in a class
Being relaxed
Being asked for my help or advice
Thinking about other people's problems
Playing board games (Monopoly, Scrabble, etc.)
Sleeping soundly at night
Doing heavy outdoor work (cutting or chopping wood, cleaning land, farm work, etc.)
Reading the newspaper
Snowmobiling or dune-buggy riding
Being in an encounter, therapy, or "rap" group
Dreaming at night
Playing Ping-Pong
Brushing my teeth
Swimming
Running, jogging, or doing gymnastics, fitness, or field exercise
Walking barefoot
Playing Frisbee or catch
Doing housework or laundry; cleaning things
Listening to music
Debating an interesting topic
Knitting, crocheting, embroidery, or fancy needlework
Amusing people
Going to a barber
Having house guests
Reading magazines
Sleeping late
Starting a new project
Being stubborn
Going to the library
Playing soccer, rugby, hockey, lacrosse, etc.

Preparing a new or special food
Bird watching
Shopping
Watching people
Building or watching a fire
Winning an argument
Selling or trading something
Finishing a project or task
Repairing things
Working with others as a team
Bicycling
Being with happy people
Playing party games
Writing letters, cards, or notes
Talking about politics or public affairs
Asking for help or advice
Going to banquets, luncheons, potlucks, etc.
Talking about my hobby or special interest
Smiling at people
Playing sand, a stream, the grass, etc.
Talking about other people
Being with my husband or wife
Playing with pets
Going on field trips, nature walks, etc.
Expressing my love to someone
Caring for houseplants
Having coffee, tea, a coke, etc., with friends
Taking a walk
Collecting things
Playing handball, paddleball, squash, etc.
Going to a play
Remembering a departed friend or loved one, visiting the cemetery
Beachcombing
Being complimented or told I have done well
Looking at the stars or moon
Eating snacks
Staying up late
Having family members or friends do something that makes me proud of them
Being with my children
Going to auctions, garage sales, etc.
Thinking about an interesting question
Doing volunteer work, working on community service projects
Water skiing, surfing, scuba diving
Being coached
Defending or protecting someone; stopping fraud or abuse

Hearing a good sermon
Winning a competition
Making a new friend
Talking about my job or school
Reading cartoons, comic strips, or comic books
Borrowing something
Traveling with a group
Seeing old friends
Teaching someone
Using my strength
Traveling
Going to office parties or departmental get-togethers
Attending a concert, opera, or ballet
Helping the elderly
Participate in a Community 5K Run/Walk

Appendix C

Communication: Speaker-Listener Checklist

1. Use "I" statements.
2. Talk about feelings and concerns in short, clear statements.
3. Pause after paraphrasing, seek understanding.
4. Praise speaker when they paraphrase correctly and ask them to clarify when they don't.
5. Give the other the floor every few statements.
6. Keep opinions to yourself until you have the floor.
7. Use validation and compliments often.
8. Ask for examples or specifics.
9. Don't be afraid to ask the speaker to qualify their statements.
10. If heated or emotional, calm down then come back to the subject.

Appendix D

The Addiction Inventory ©

Yes or No

Do you feel that your compulsive behavior is abnormal?
Were you abused in any way as a child or adolescent?
Have you ever worried about people finding out about your addictive activities?
Do you have to hide some of your behaviors from others?
Have your activities interfered with your family life?
Do you worry that your thoughts and/or behaviors are more powerful than you?
Is your addictive behavior inconsistent with your values?
Do you fantasize often about your addiction?
Do you think about it either more or less that you would like to?
Do you spend more money than you can afford to spend on it?
Does your pursuit of it interfere with normal relations with your spouse or significant others?
Have you been arrested for it?
If not arrested, then at least in some sort of trouble for it, if caught or if it got out of hand?
Have you ever felt degraded by, or felt bad about, it?
Does your partner refuse to participate in certain activities with you?
Does your addictive thoughts/behaviors interfere with your spiritual or religious life?
Do you find yourself looking for stimuli of your addiction in media outlets such as magazines, television, or internet?
Have you ever tried to stop it?
Have you ever promised yourself/someone else that you would change your behavior?
Have you broken these promises?
Have you repeatedly tried to stop what is wrong with the behavior?
Have you ever risked legal problems because of your behavior?
Do you learn about your addiction?
Do you wish you wouldn't give into it?
Does anyone get hurt (physically or emotionally) because of your activities?
Has your pursuit of it become more compulsive?
Are you at risk, or have you ever been tested or treated for a sexually transmitted disease?
Has your addiction driven you to be with persons, do things, or go places you usually wouldn't choose?
Do you wish you didn't have such overpowering compulsions?
Have your activities been abusive to yourself or someone else?
Do you have trouble stopping your behavior when you know it is inappropriate?
Has it been a way for you to escape your problems, troubles, hurt, or pain?
Have you ever sought help for the behaviors you did not like?
Has an important relationship in your life ended because of your inability to stop it?
Do you have two standards of fidelity – one for yourself and one for others?
Has your behavior ever left you feeling anxious or depressed?
Did your parents or other extended family member have trouble with it?
Are you concerned about how much time you spend in this?
Do you keep secrets about your activities from those who are important to you?
Have your family, friends, job, or work suffered because of your activities?
Do your fantasies or activities interfere with your relationships?
Does your behavior make you feel scared or weird?
Does it take more variety or frequency of activity to bring the same level of excitement?
Do you think that your additive abilities are the most important qualities you have to offer another person?
Do your thoughts/ behaviors cause you to believe that you don't deserve to have a religious or spiritual life?
Have you ever had to lie to a loved one about your behavior?
Do you use threats or promises in order to participate in your behaviors?

The Addiction Inventory© continued

Do you sometimes think that you are the only person who has certain thoughts or engages in these behaviors?
Do you set rules regarding when, how, or with whom you can be, then break them?
Does your pursuit of this jeopardize your own welfare?
Do you wish you could stop now?
Do you fight an emotional battle almost everyday as it relates to this?
Do you find yourself asking for a miracle for this to go away?

Scoring:

Total number of yes answers________

Key:

If you answer YES to five or more of these questions, you are struggling with an addiction and need intervention. Higher numbers of YES answers indicates greater intensity of addiction.

Important Contacts

Name	Address	Phone	Email
(Sponsor)			

Journal

Journal

Journal

Journal

Journal

Journal

Journal

Journal

CPSIA information can be obtained
at www.ICGtesting.com
Printed in the USA
LVHW101232210419
614969LV00001B/6/P

9 780977 977314